Quarantine Day
Coloring Book

Large Size 8.5" x 11" inches
(21.59 x 27.94 cm.)

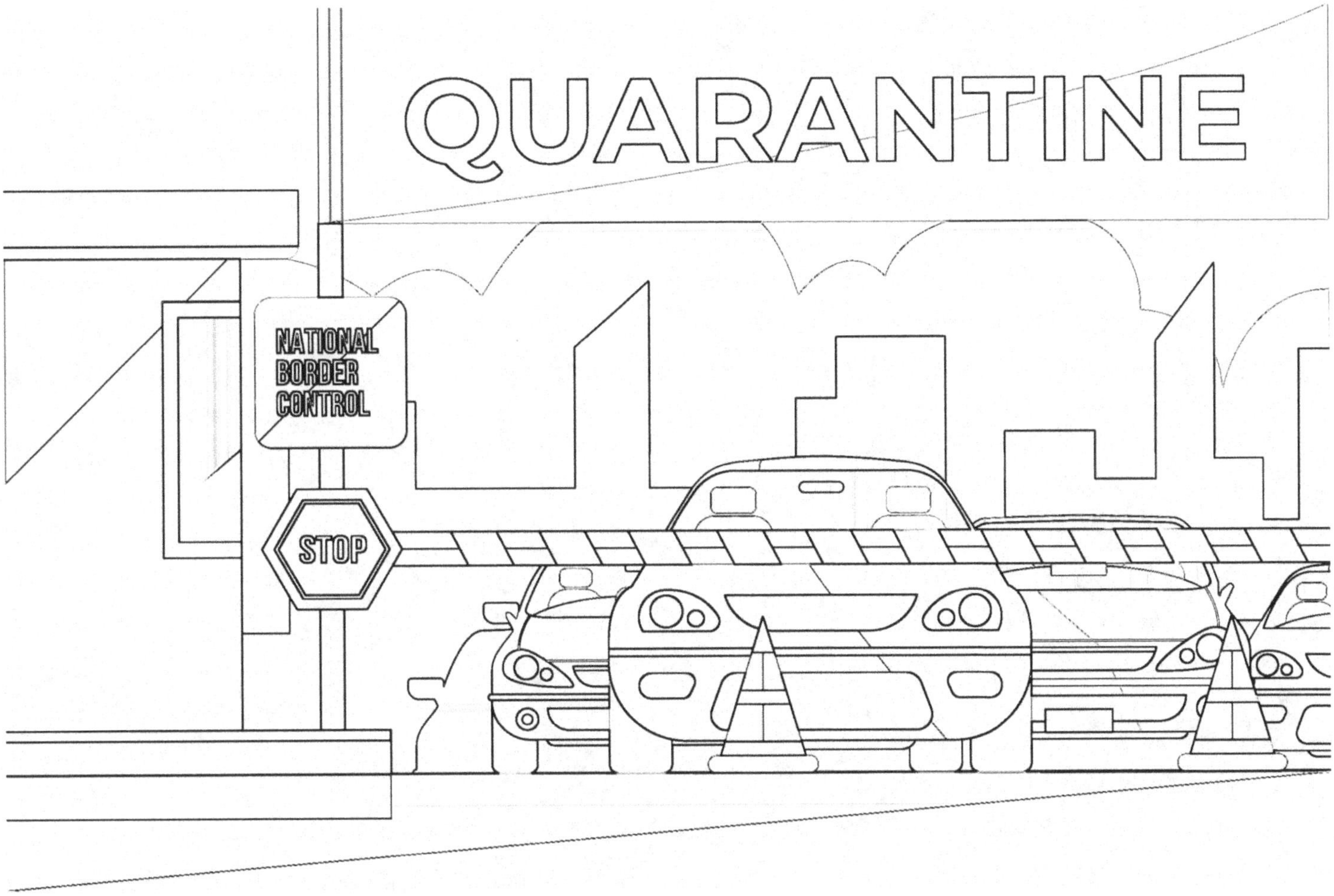

Age in Years	USA Grade	England and Wales	Scotland and Northern Ireland	Republic of Ireland
9/10	4	5	Primary 6	4th Class
10/11	5	6	Primary 7	5th Class
11/12	6	7	Secondary 1	6th Class
12/13	7	8	Secondary 2	1st Year
13/14	8	9	Secondary 3	2nd Year
14/15	9	10	Secondary 4	3rd Year
15/16	10	11	Secondary 5	4th Year
16/17	11	12	Secondary 6	5th Year
17/18	12	13	Secondary 7	6th Year

Created by Molly M. Clarke
Editor Copyright © Molly M. Clarke 2020
ISBN: 9798647259462

(For Kids Ages 10+ Years, Teens & Adults)

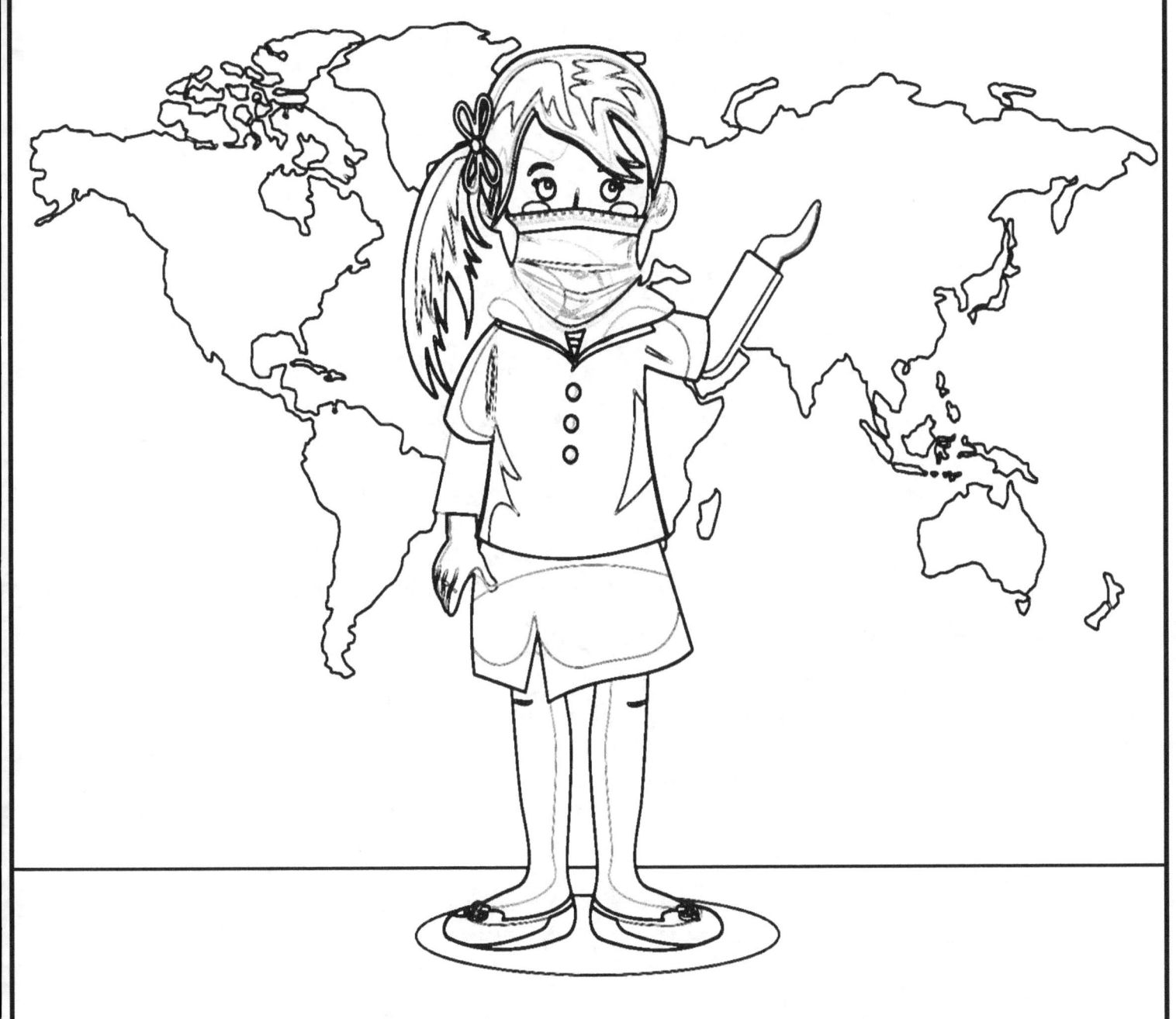

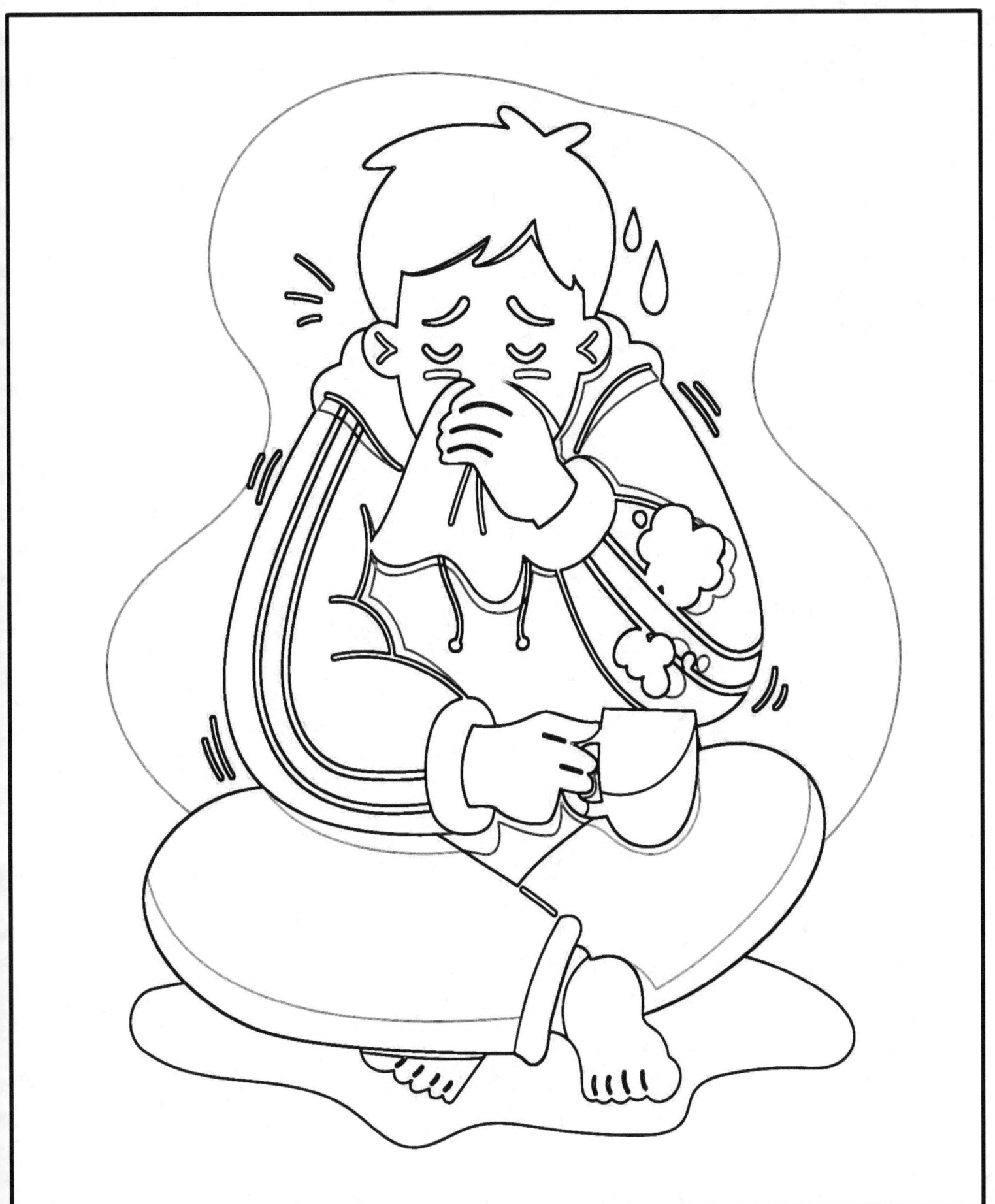

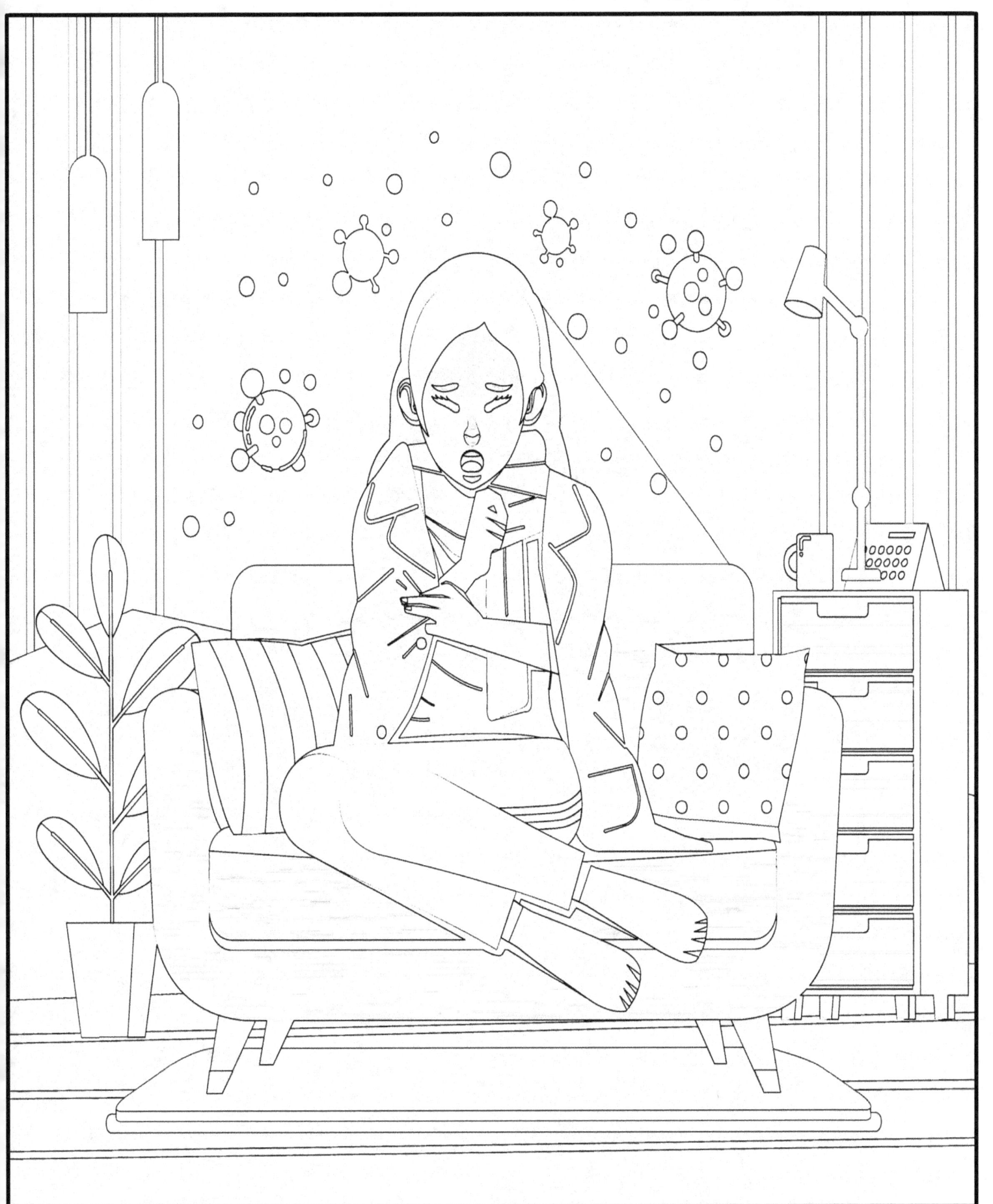

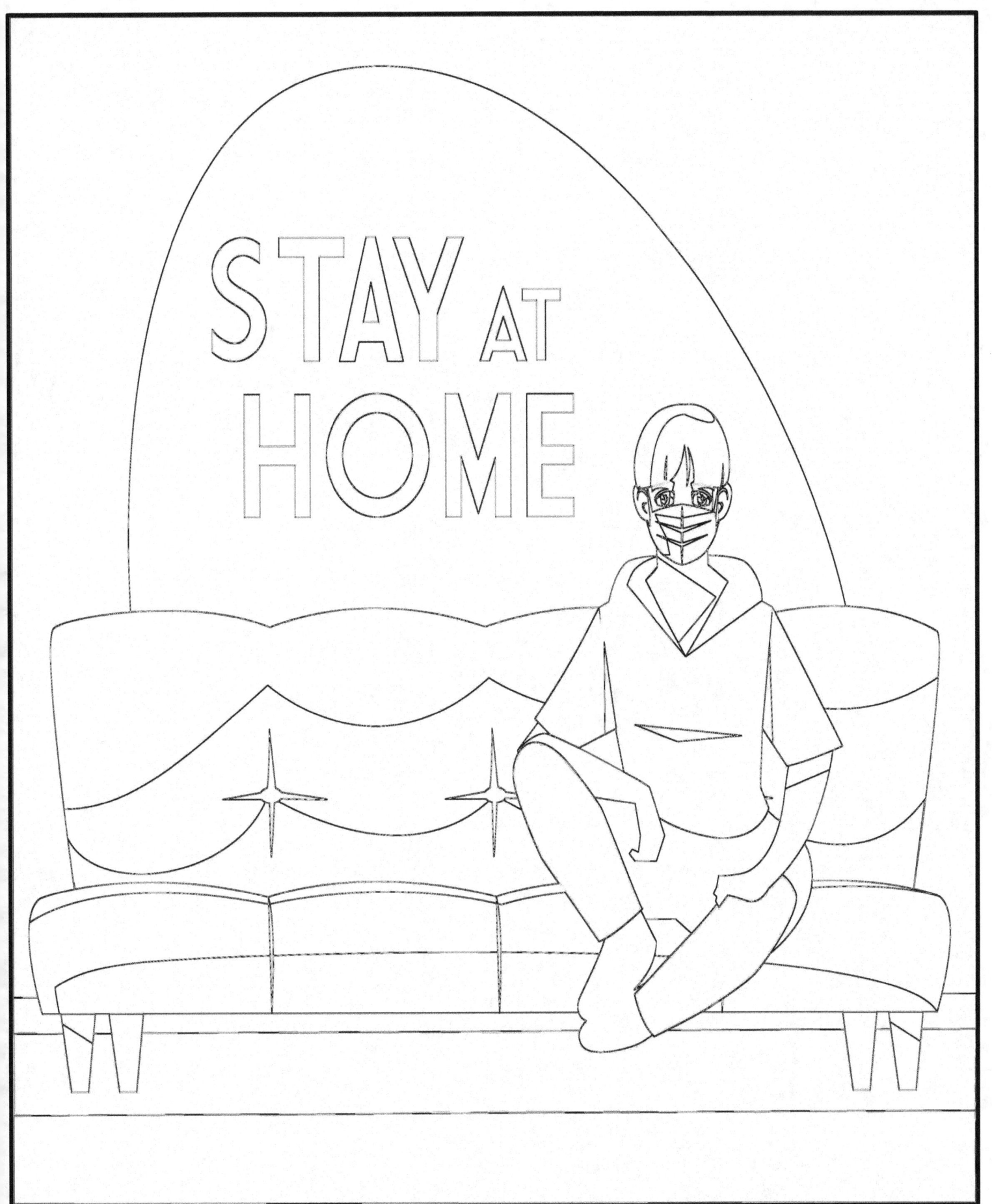

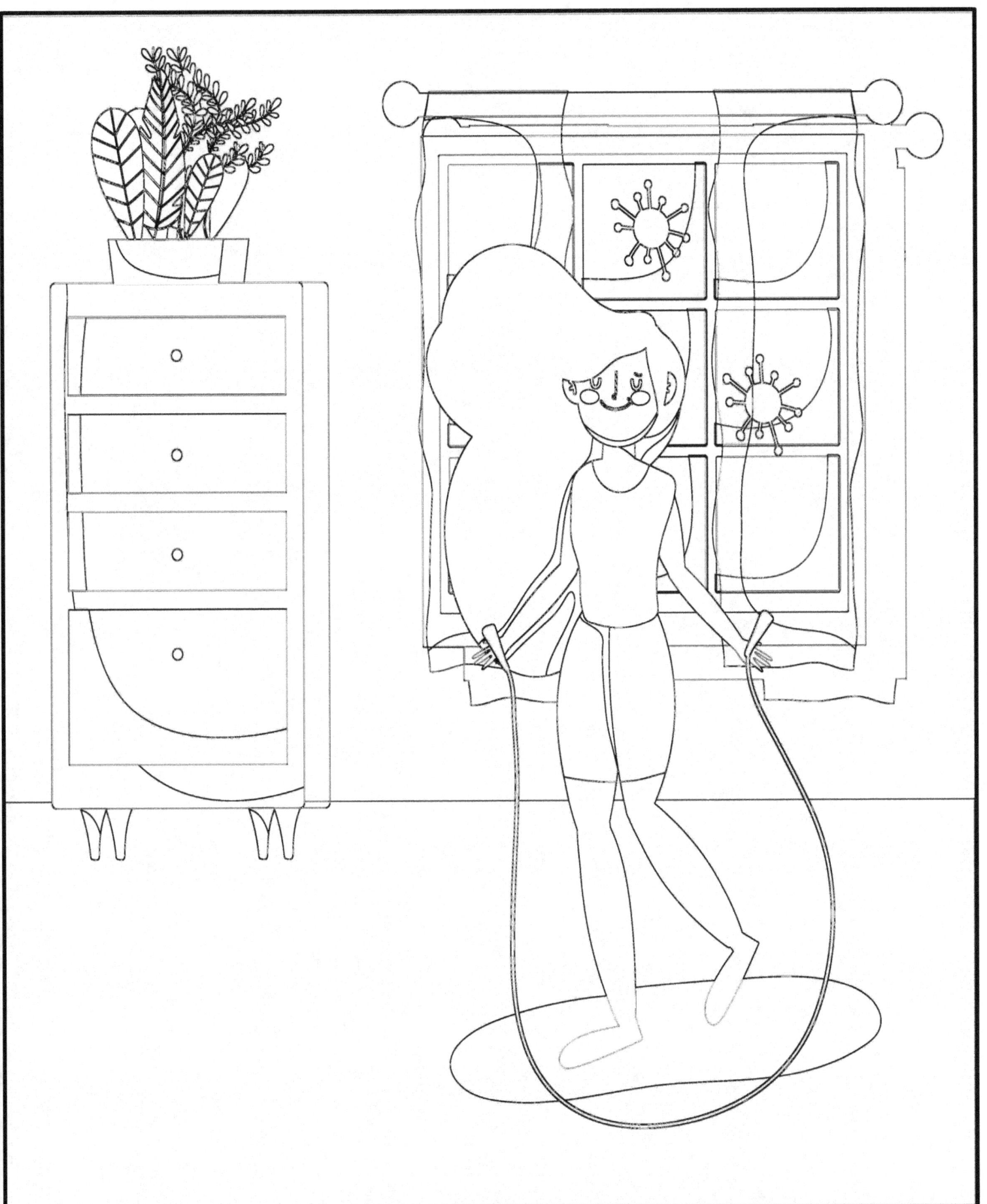

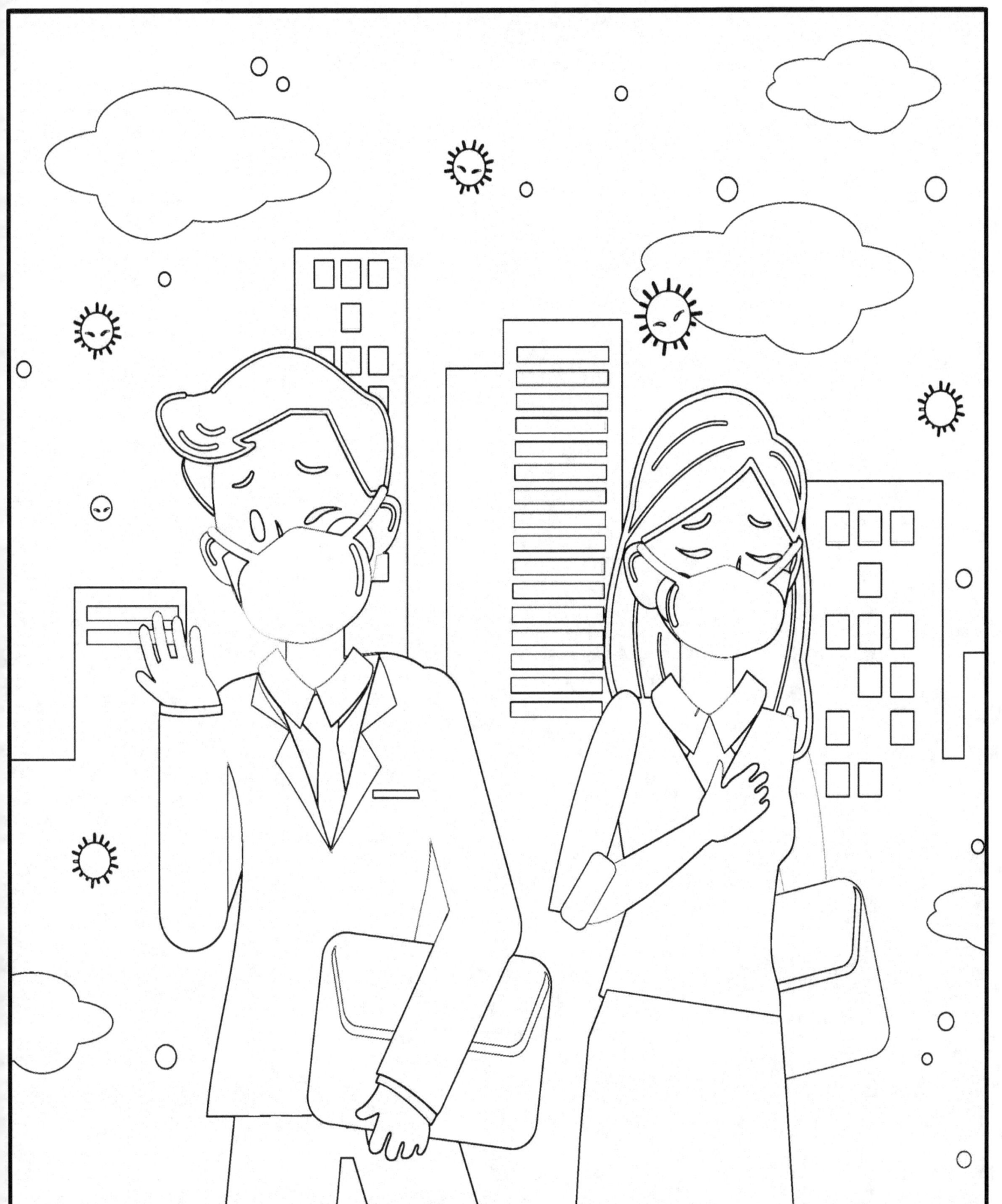

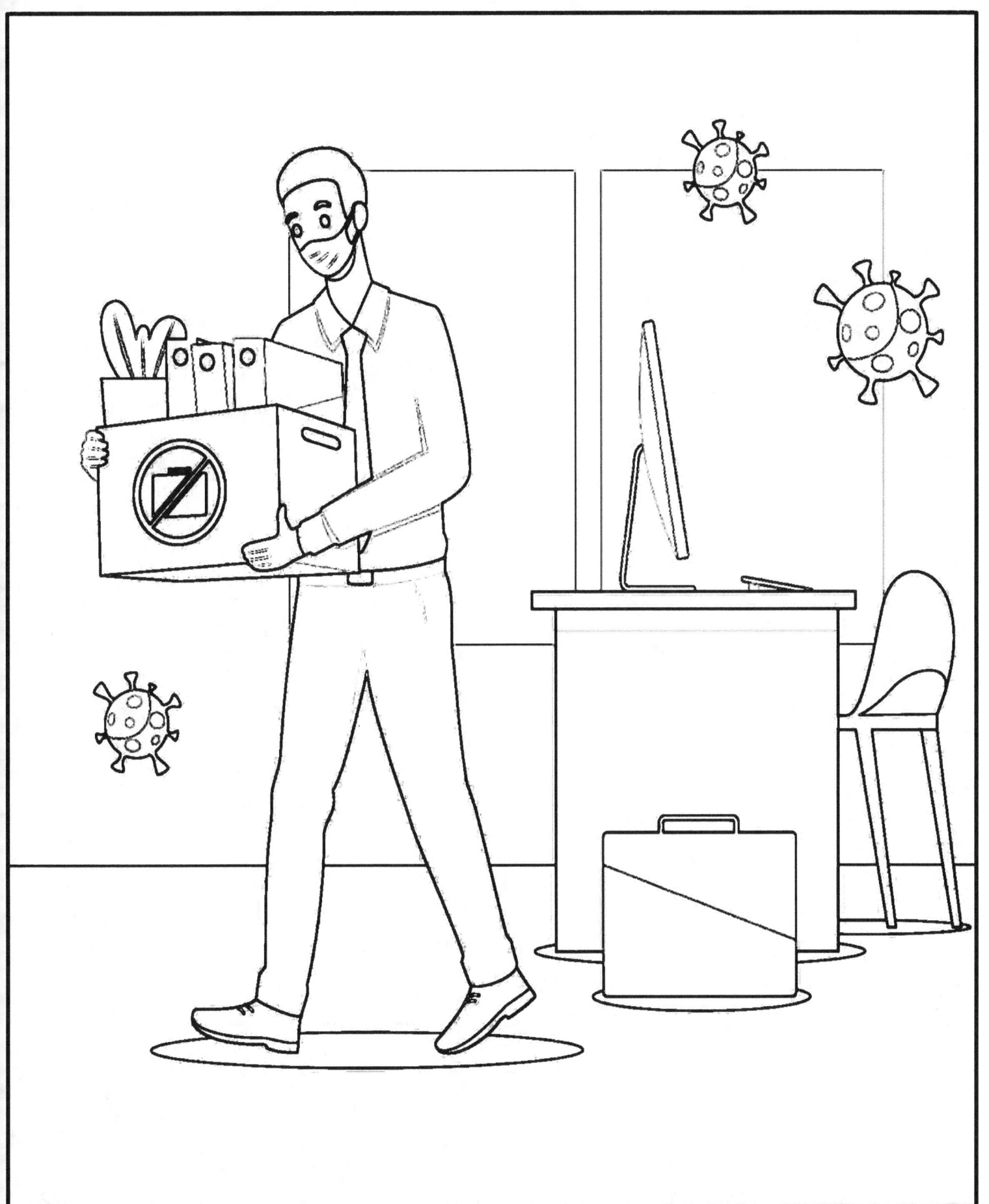

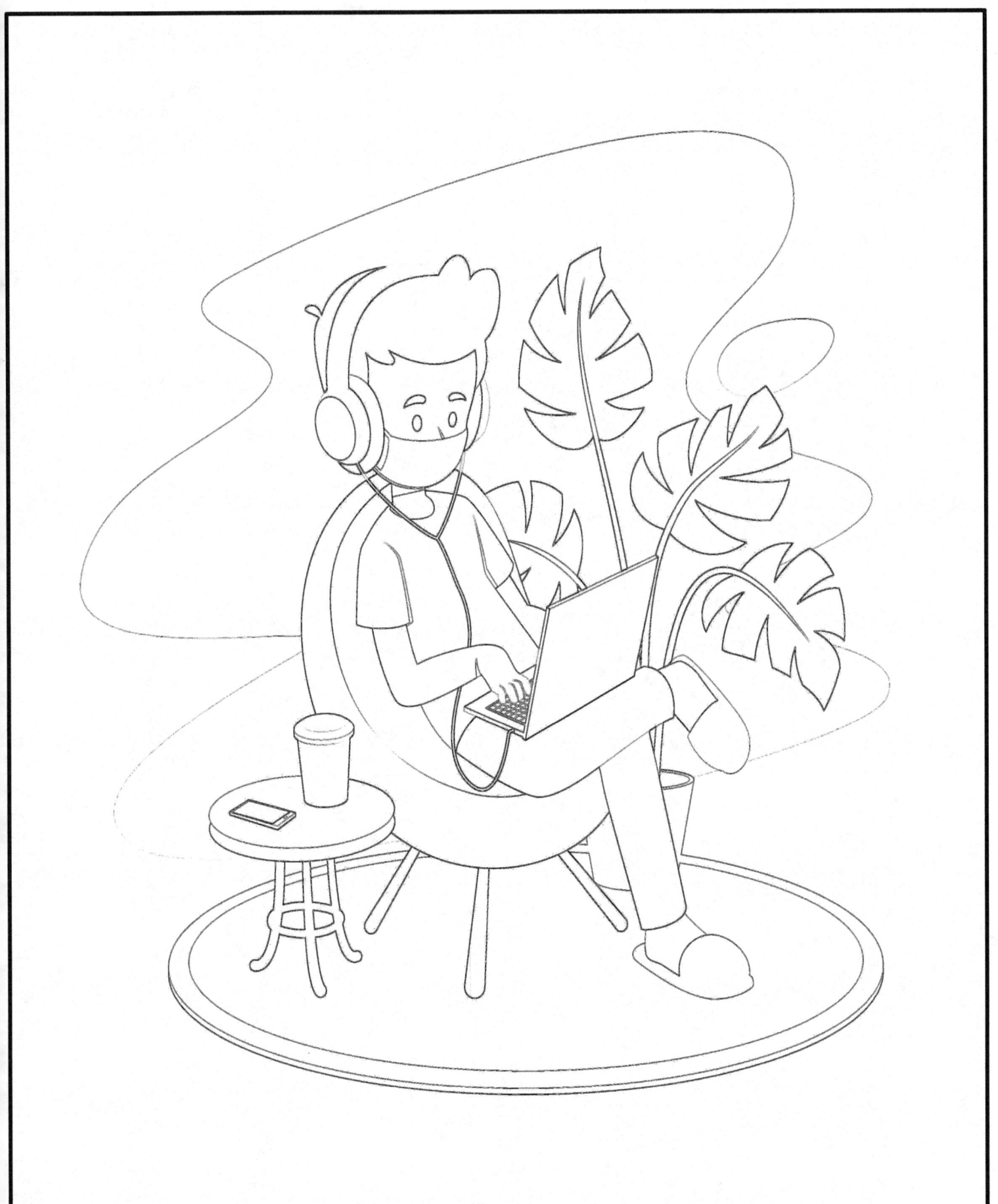

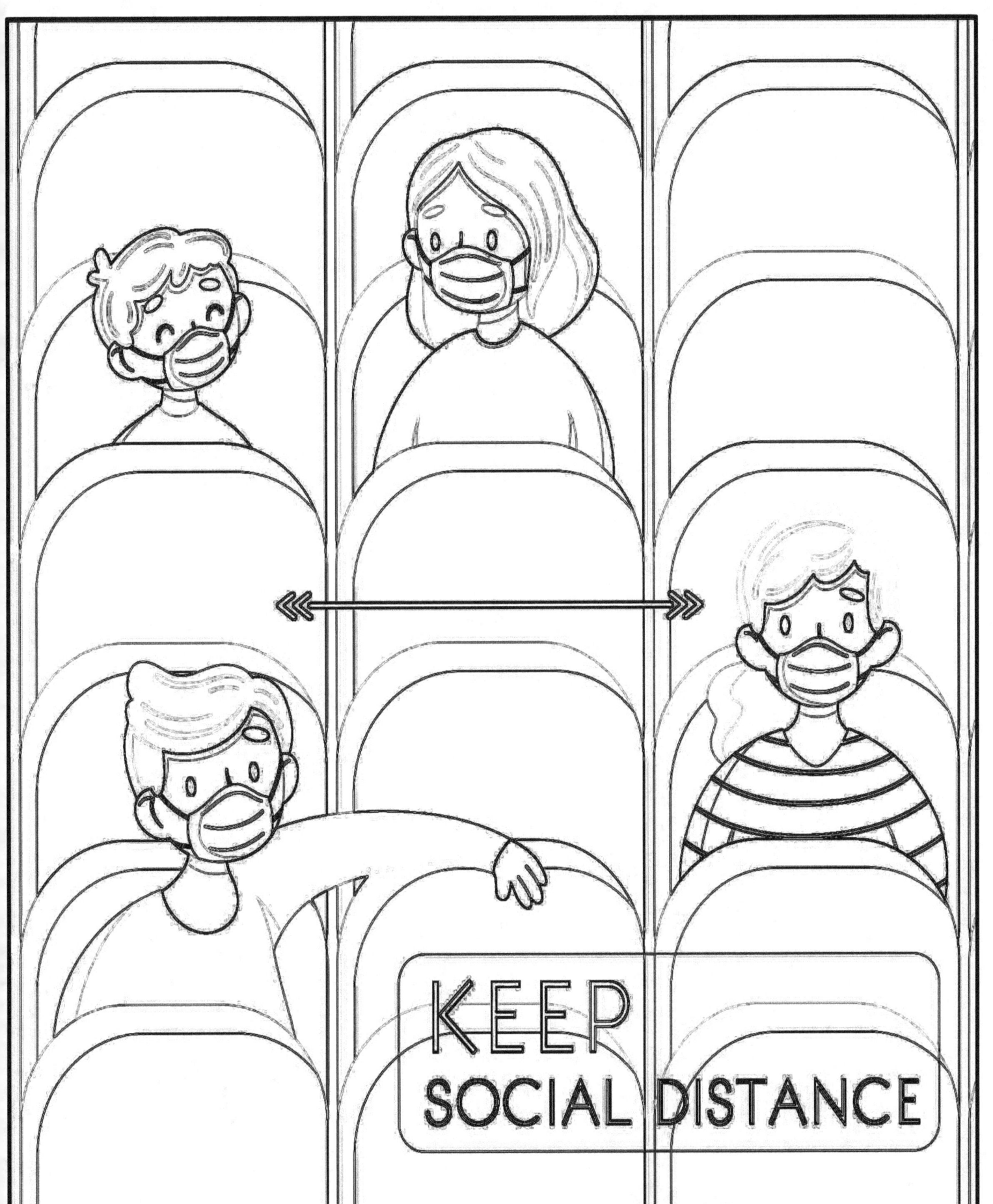

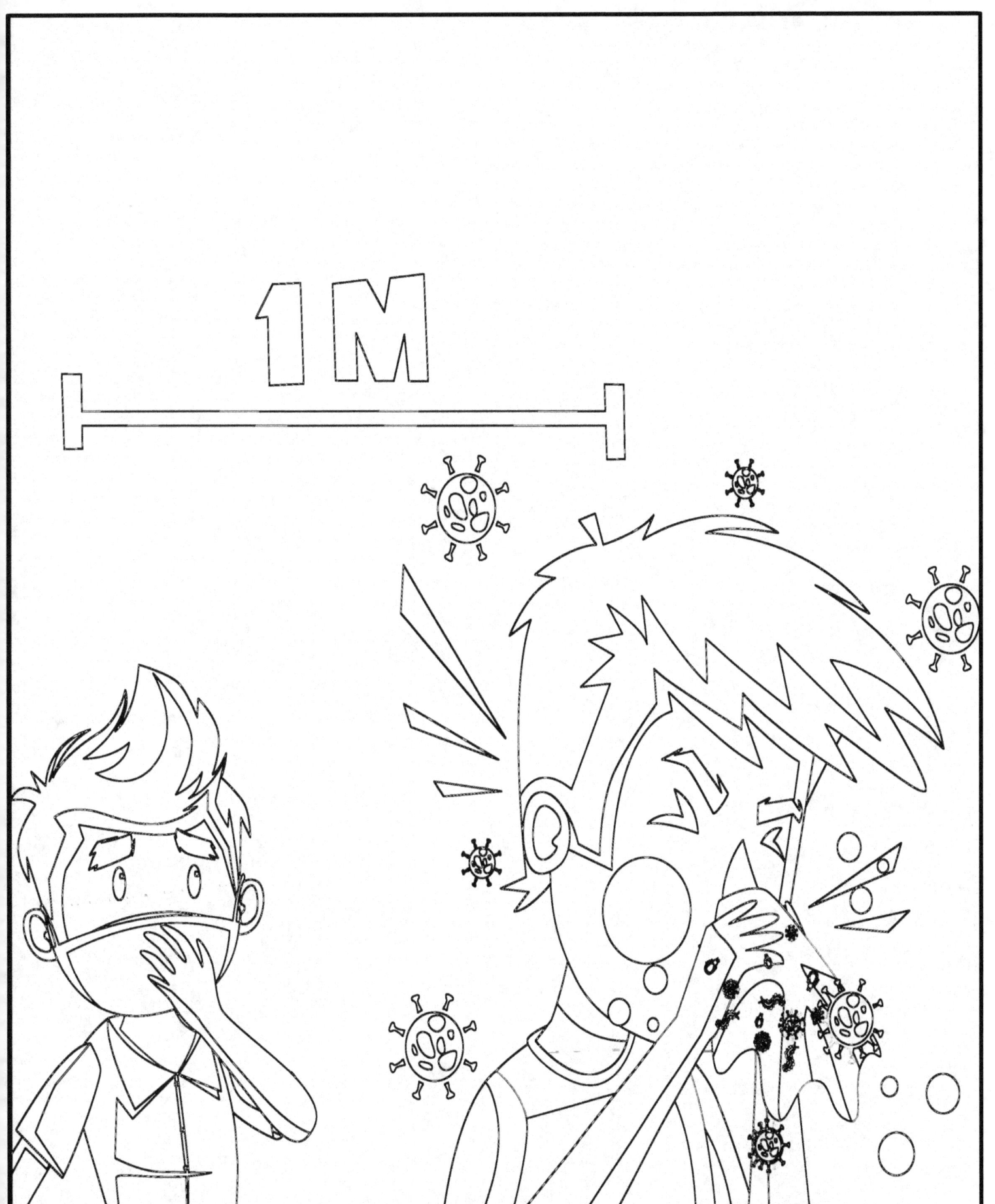

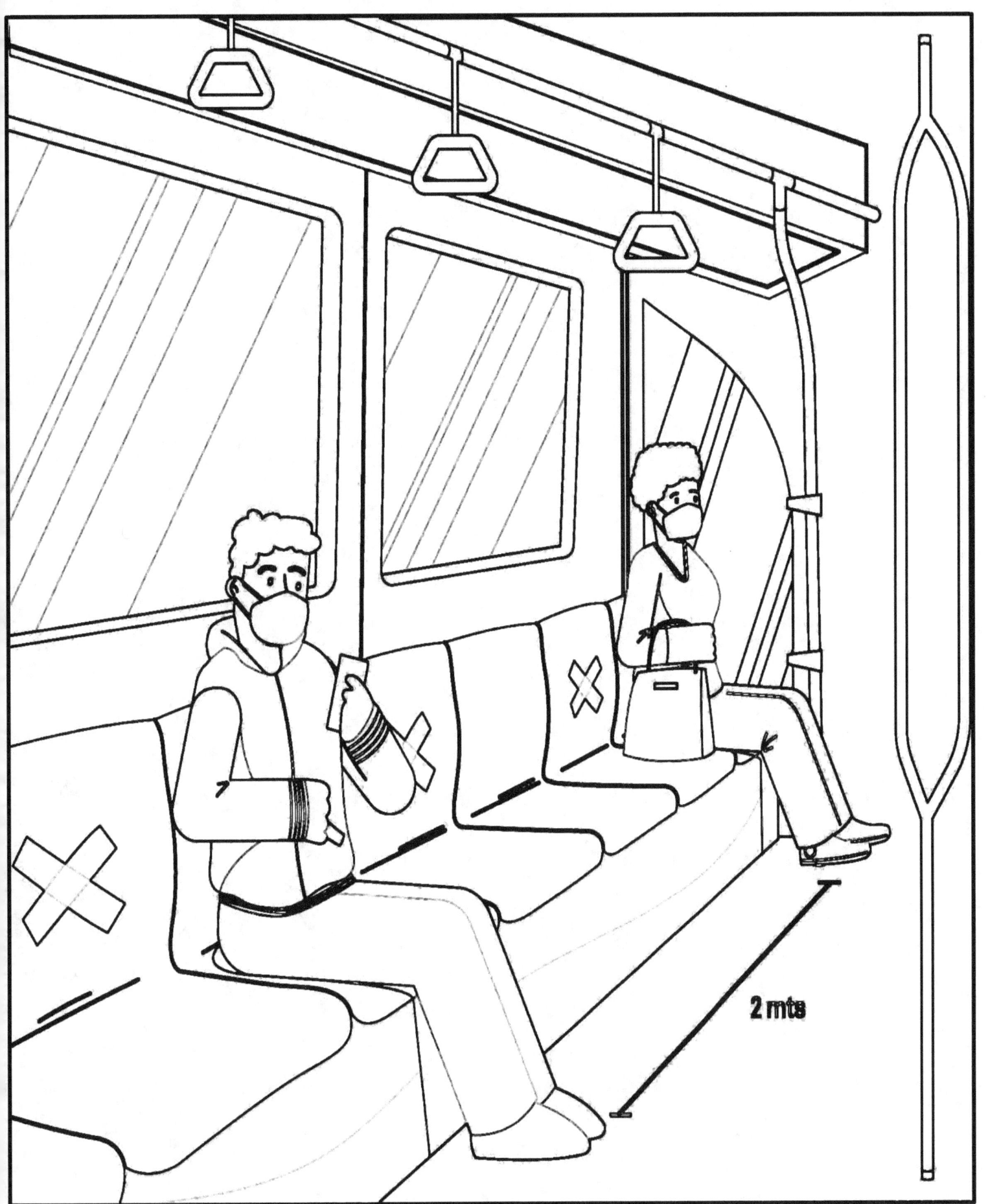

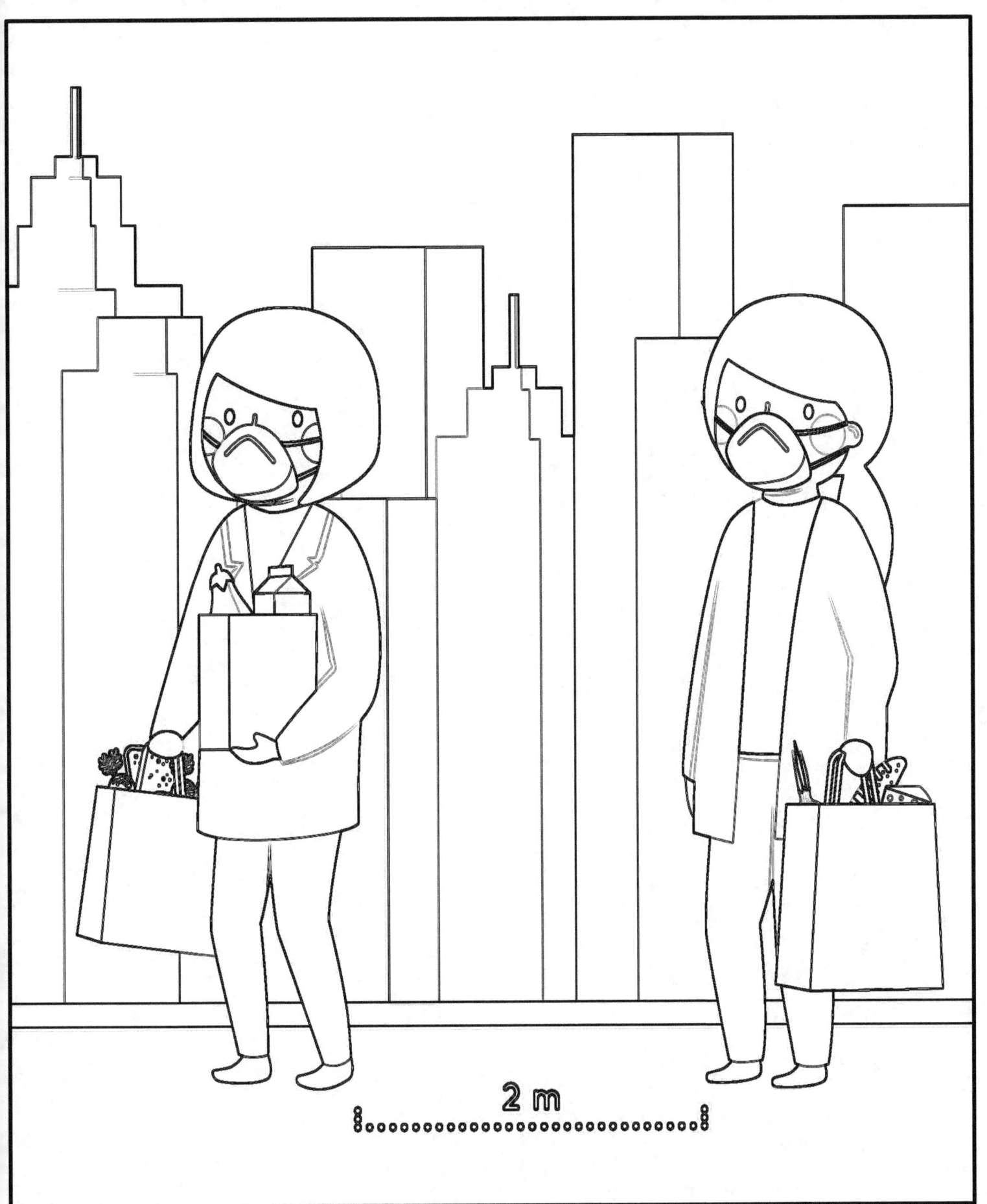

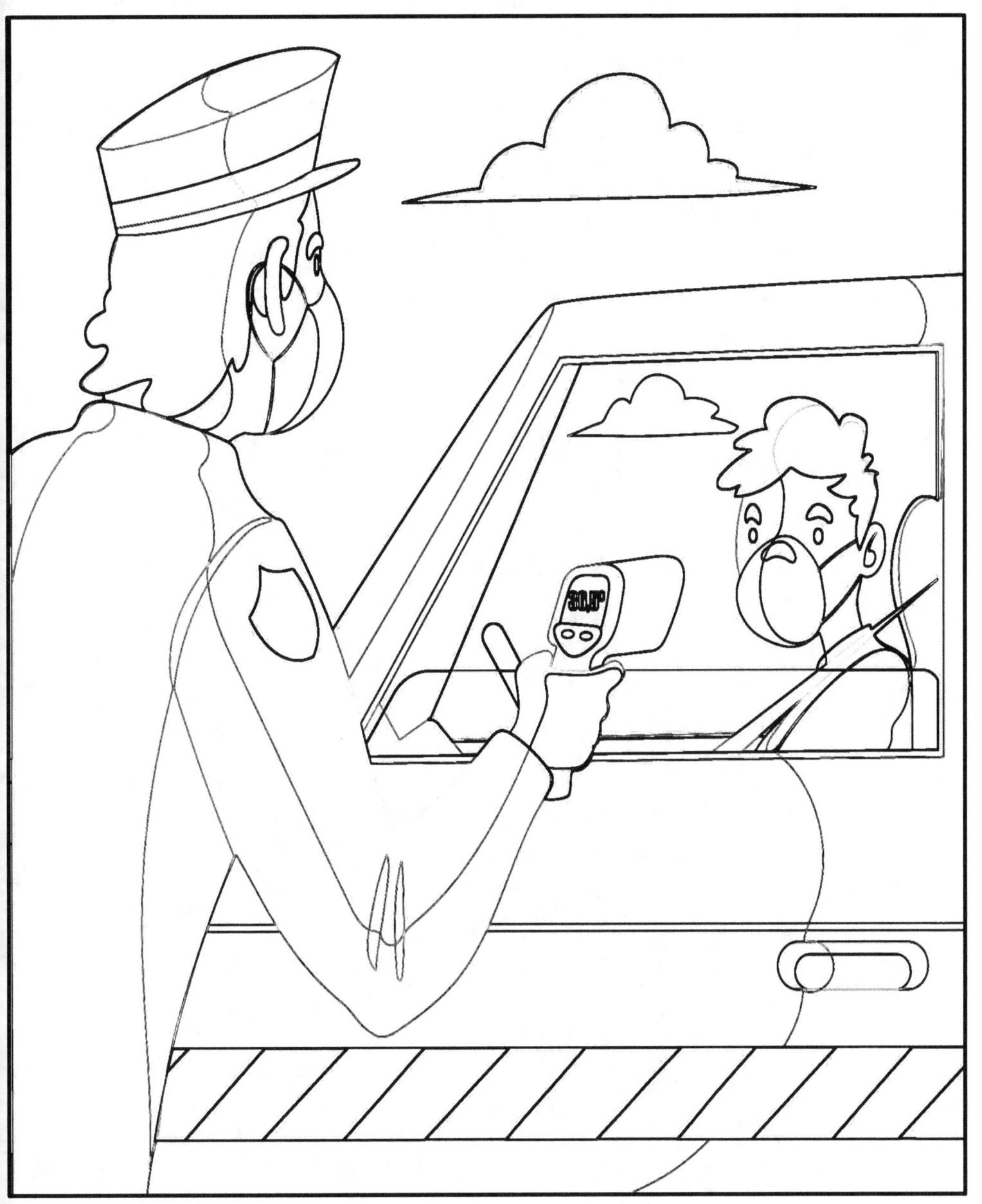

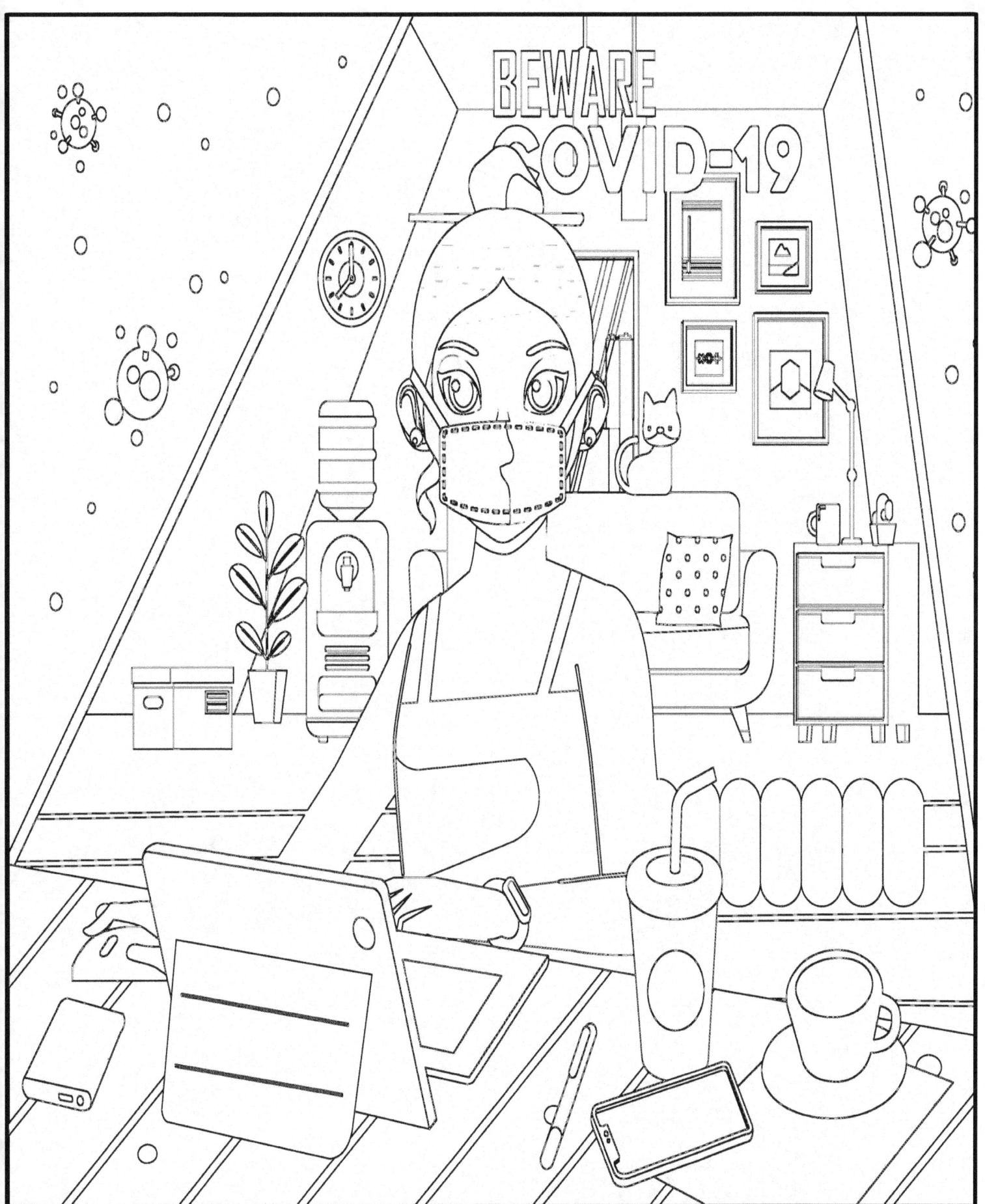

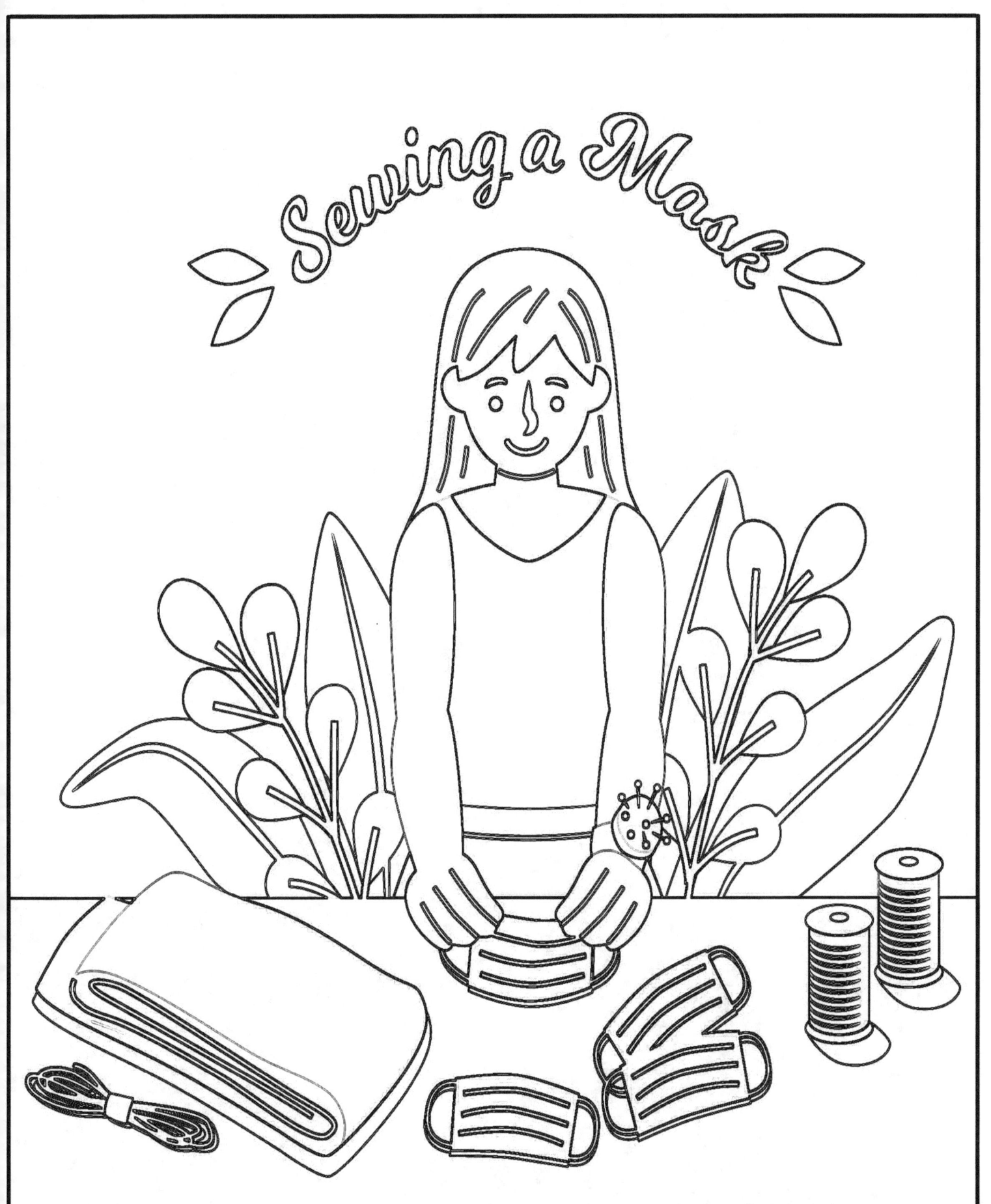

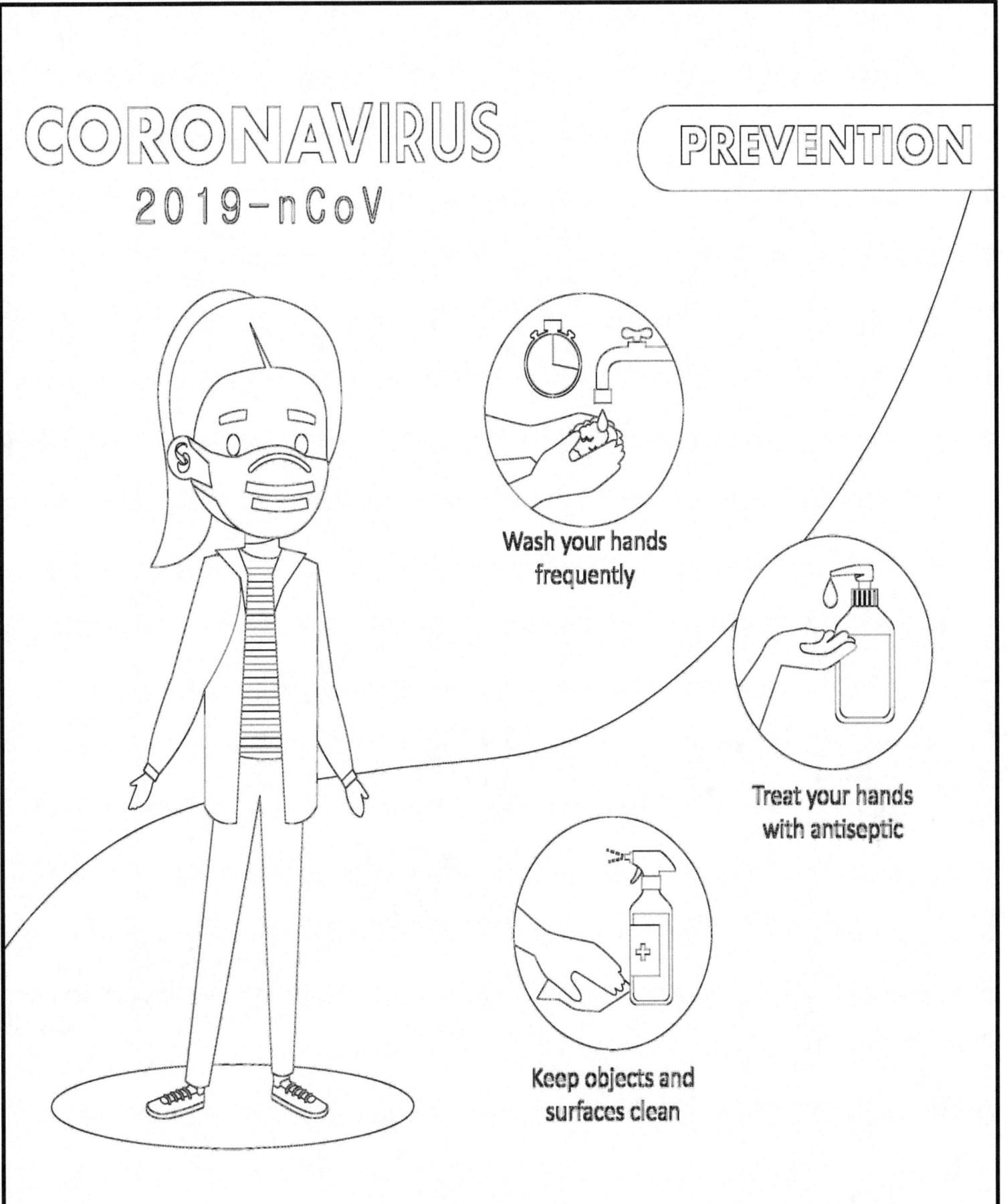

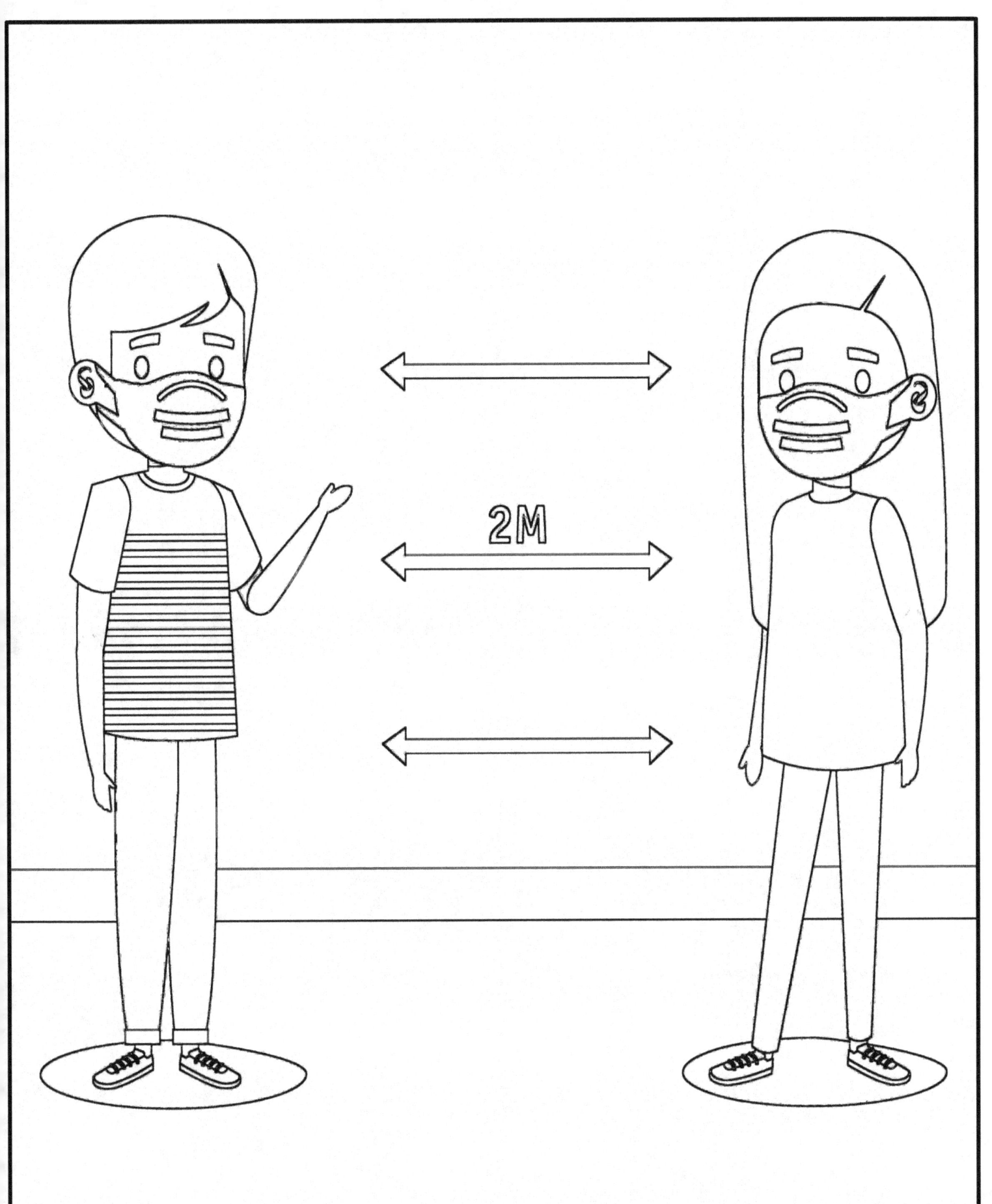

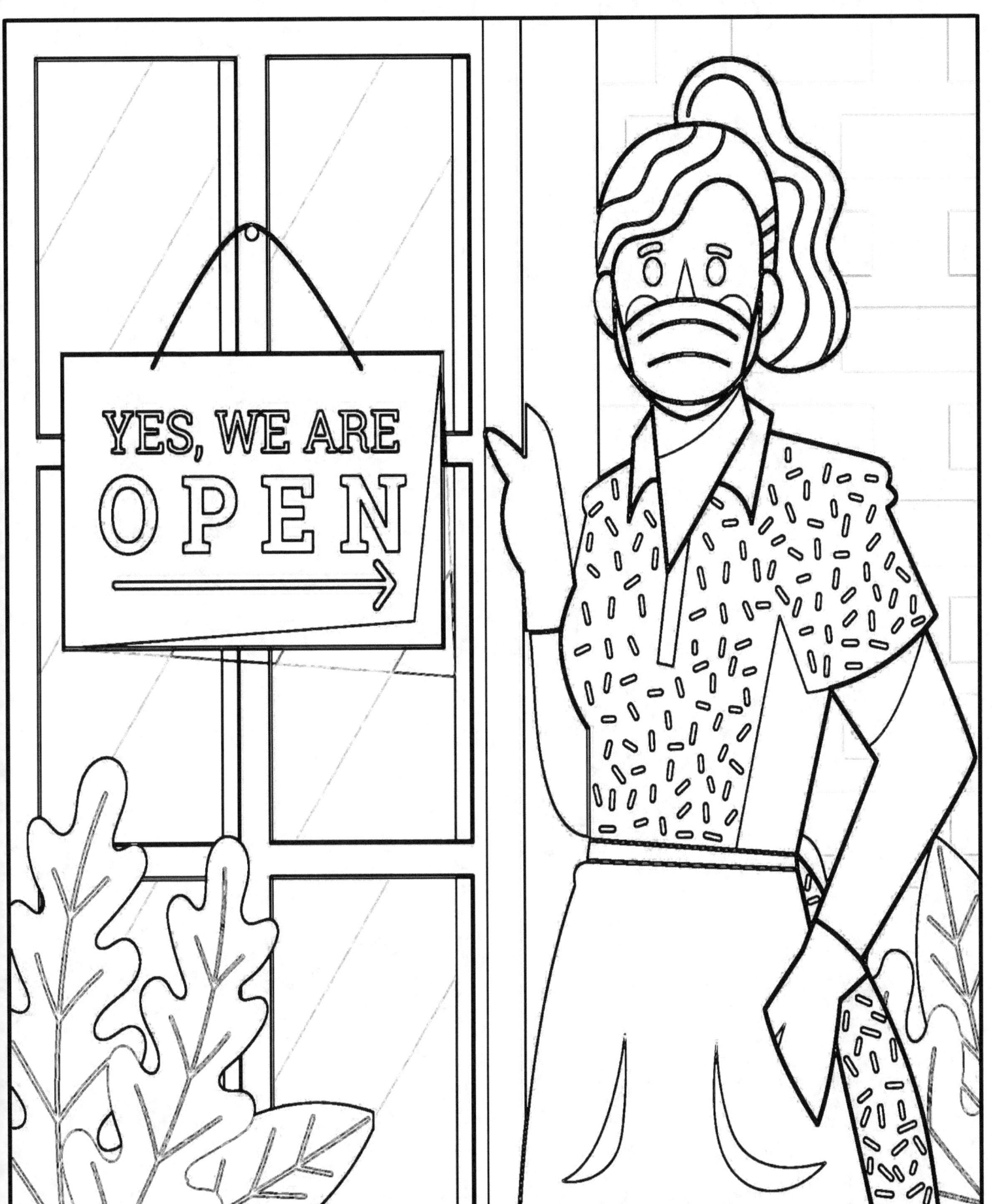

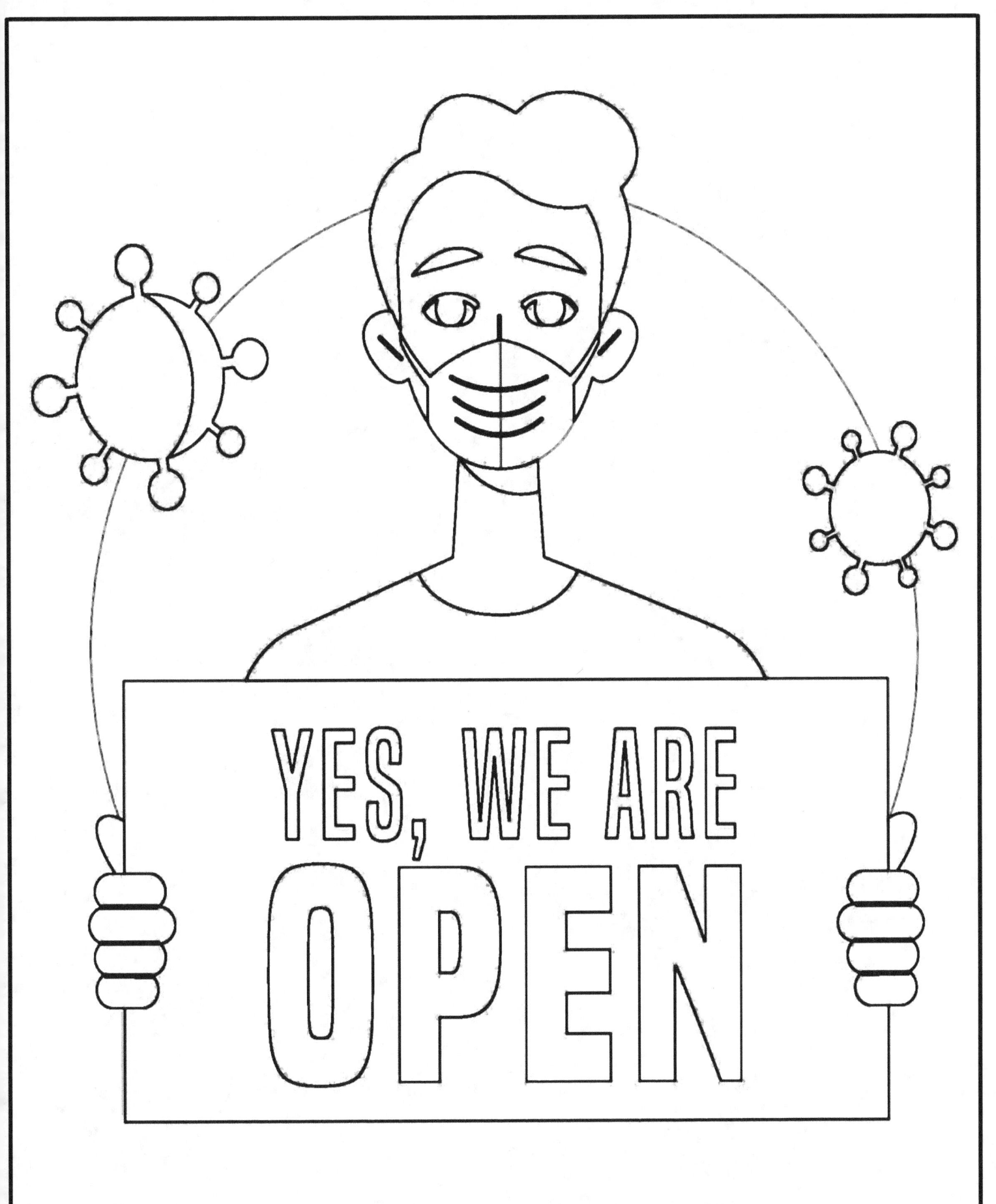

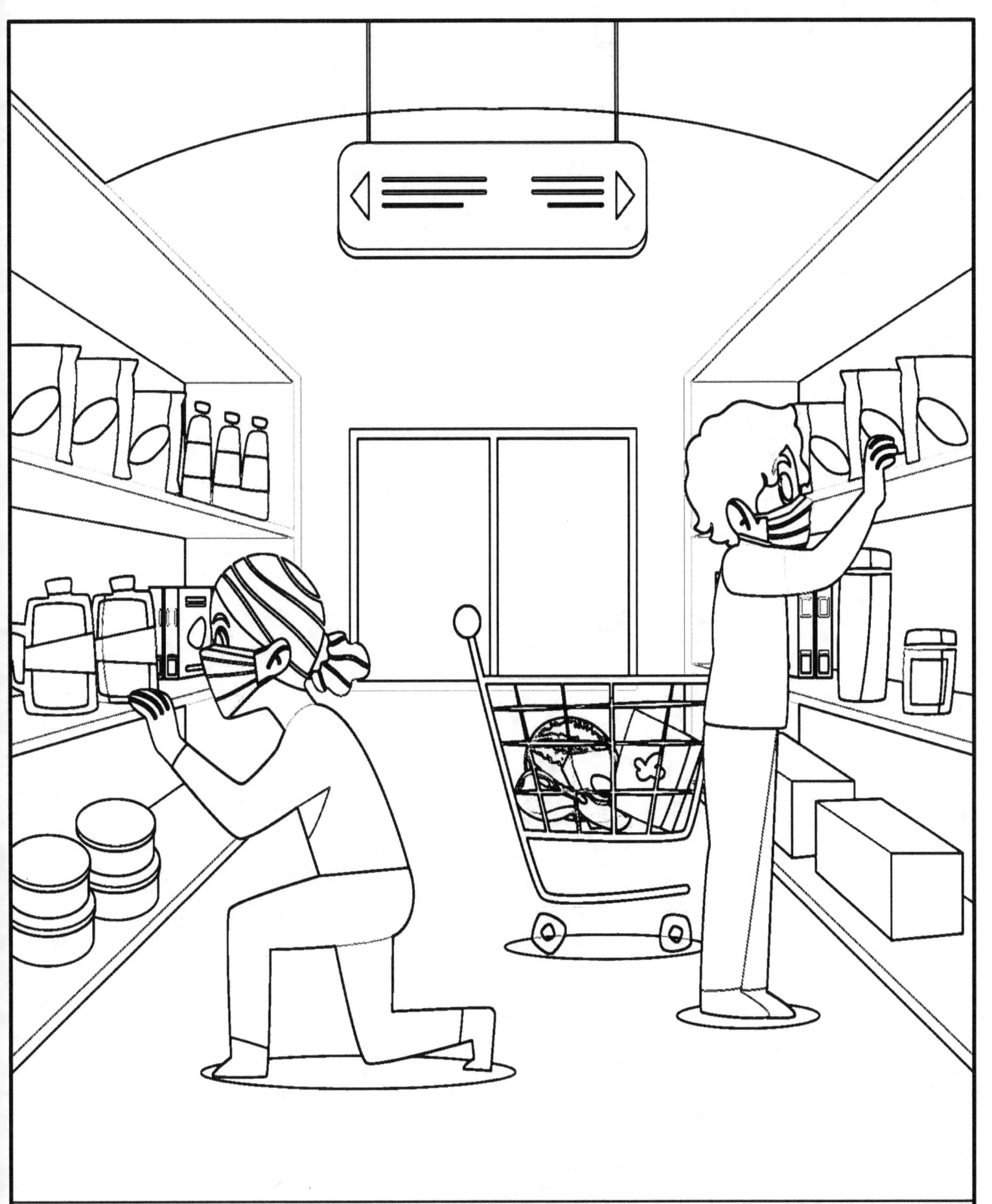

.20.

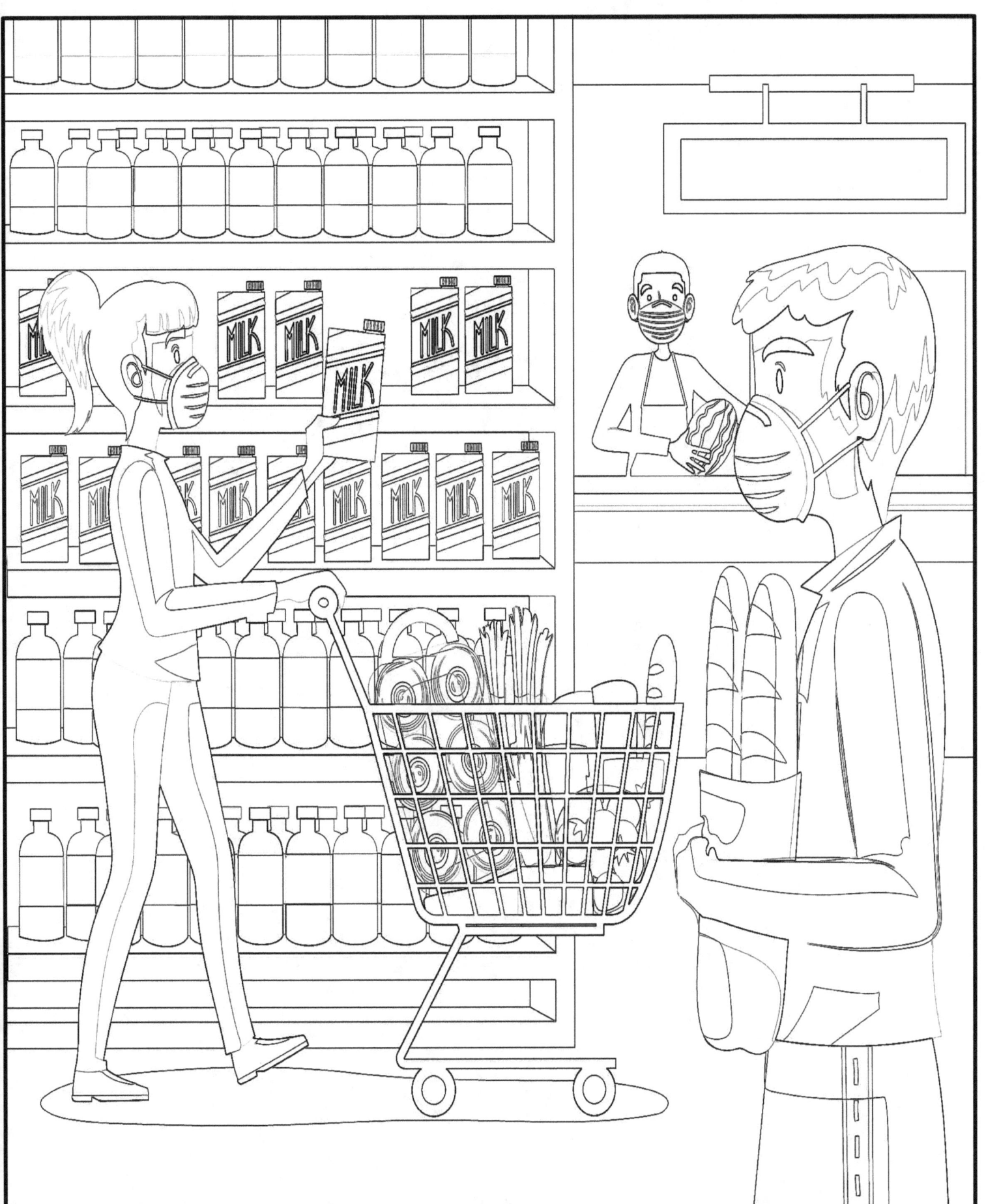

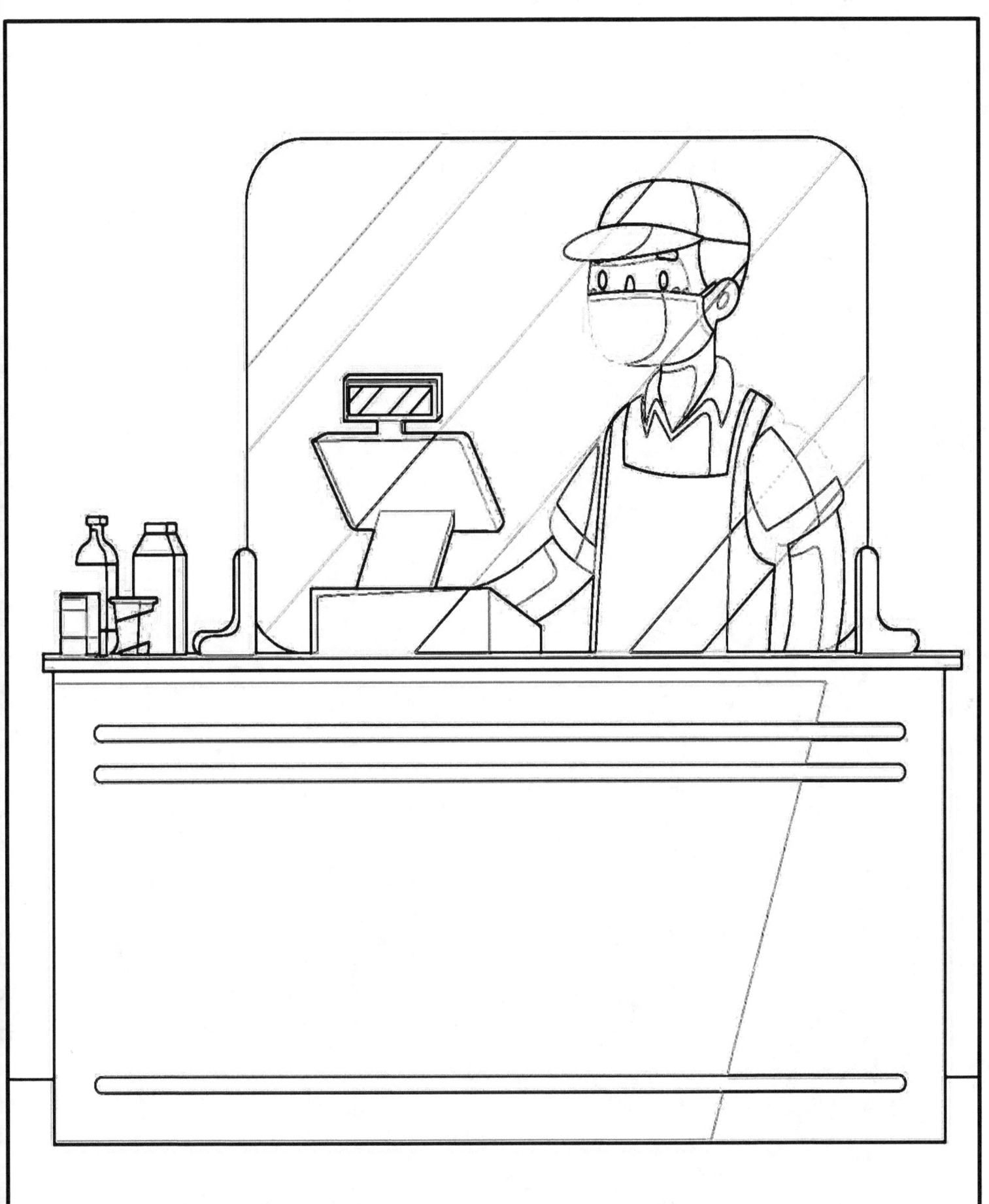

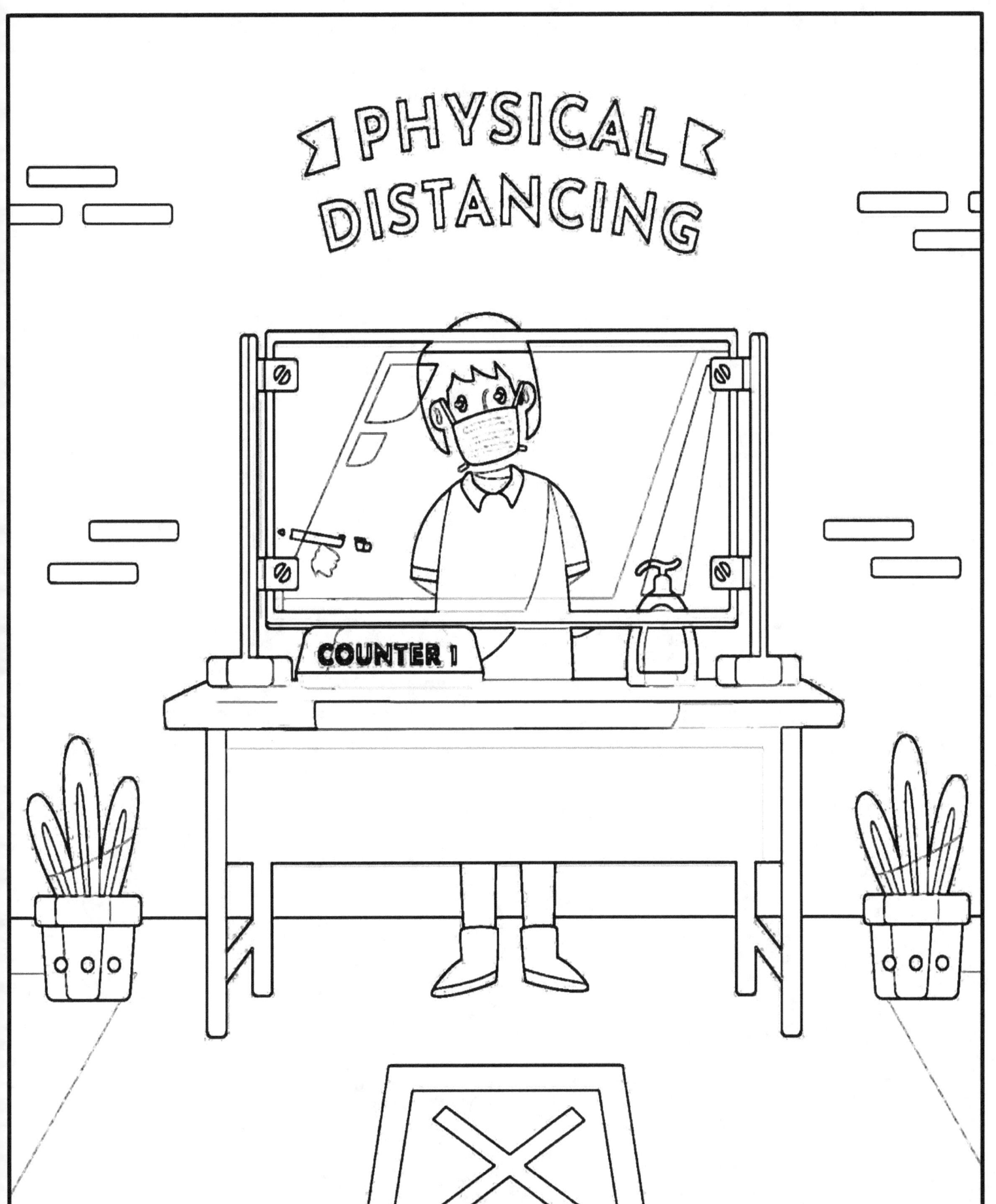

SAFE DELIVERY

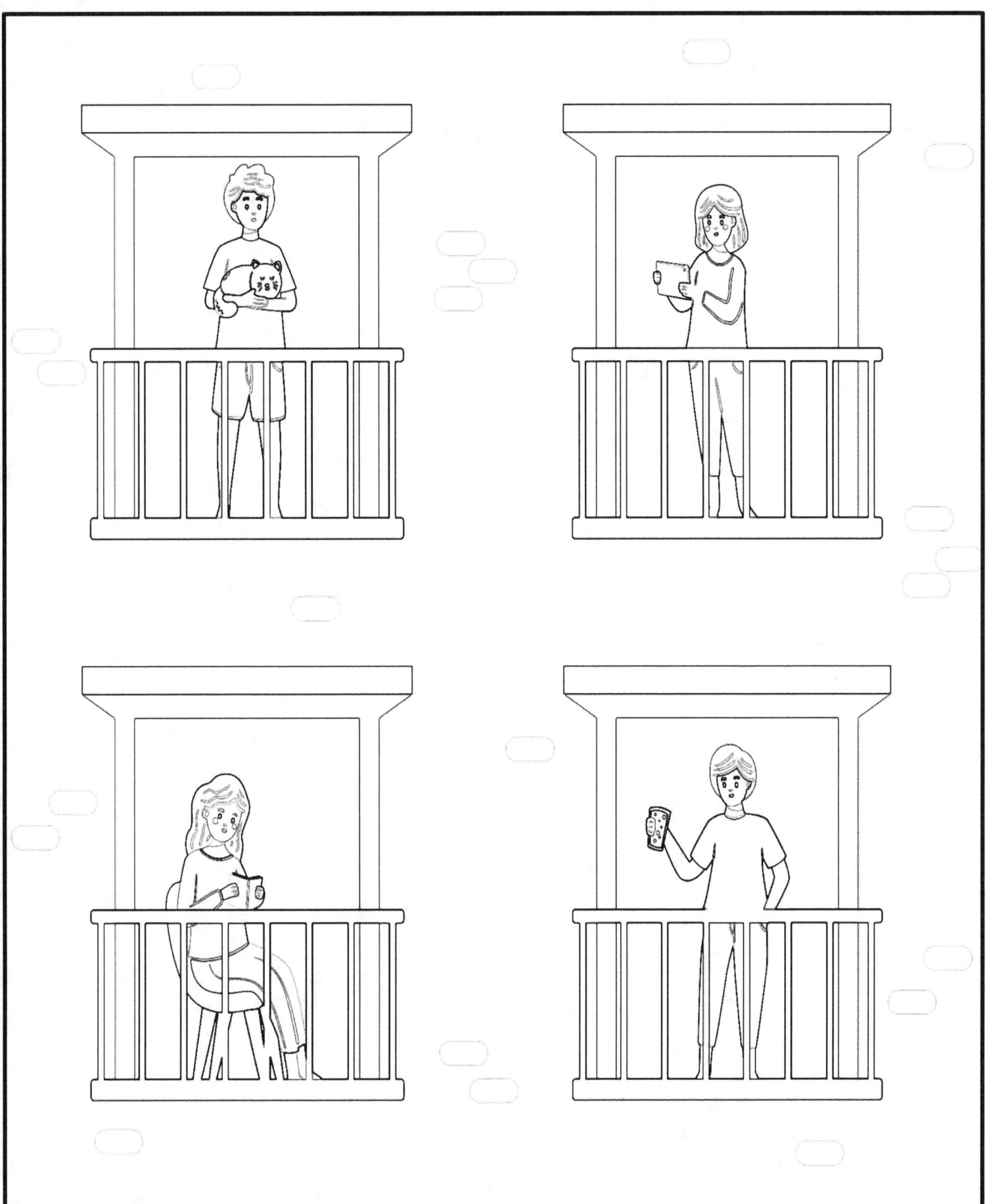

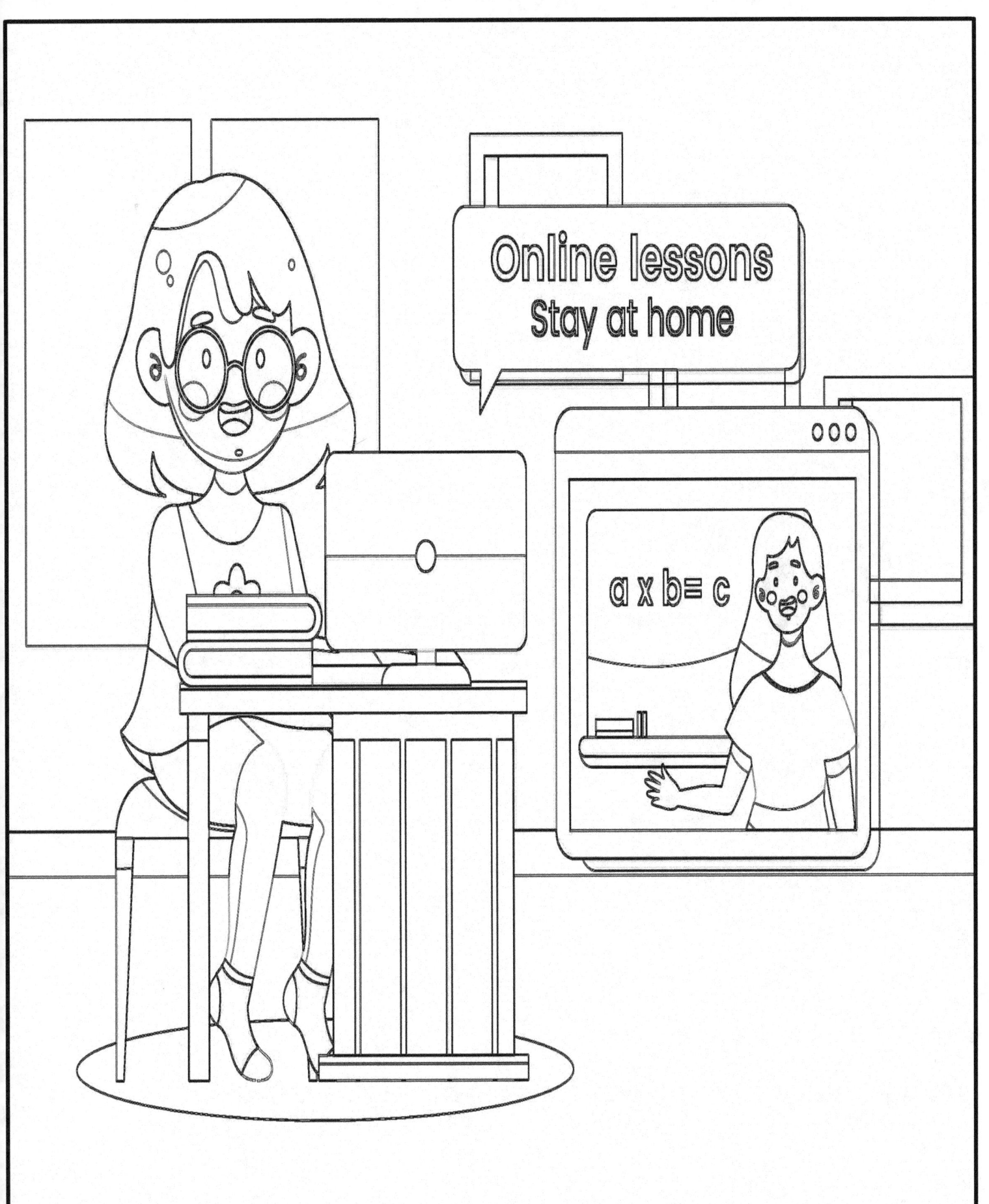

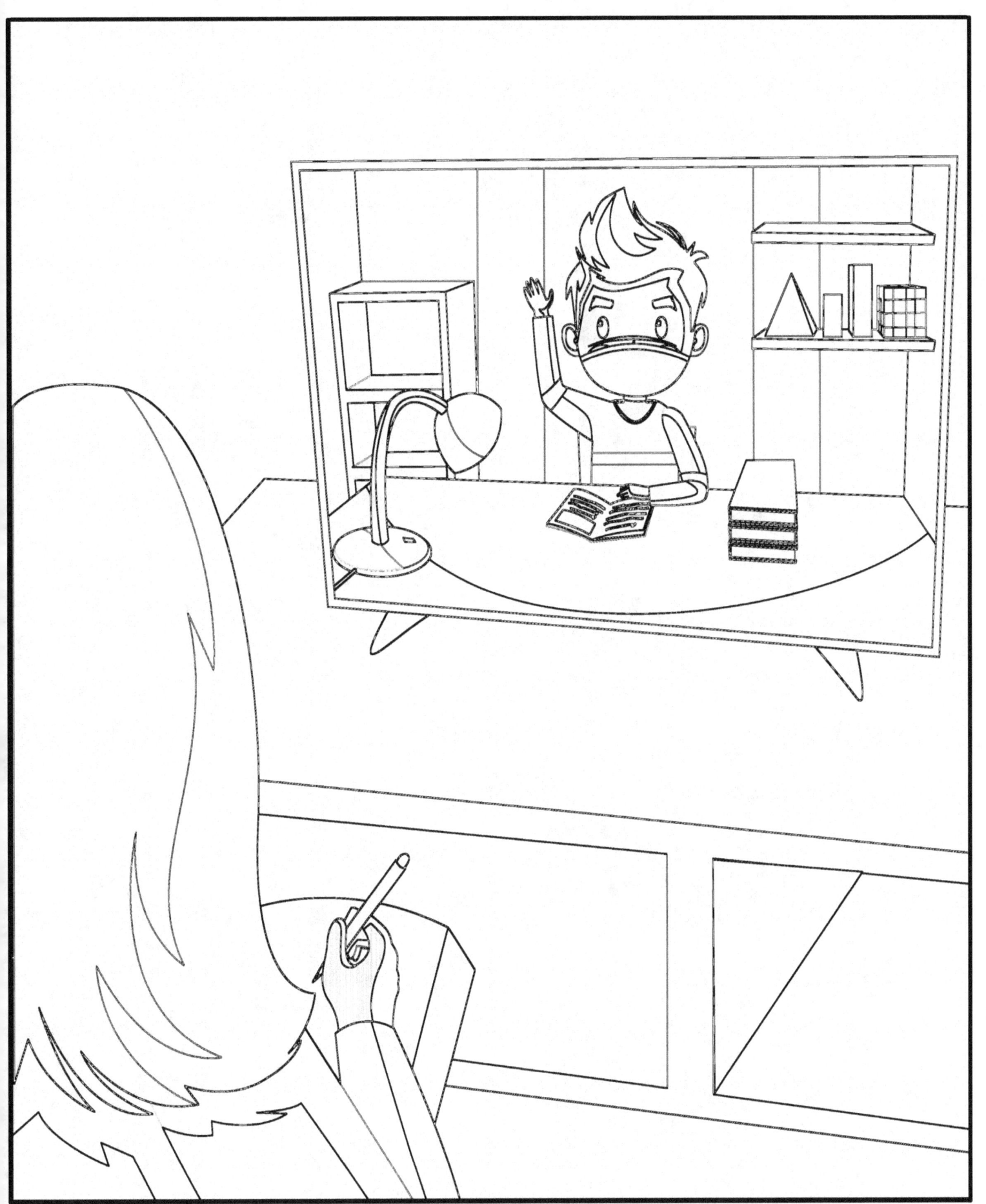

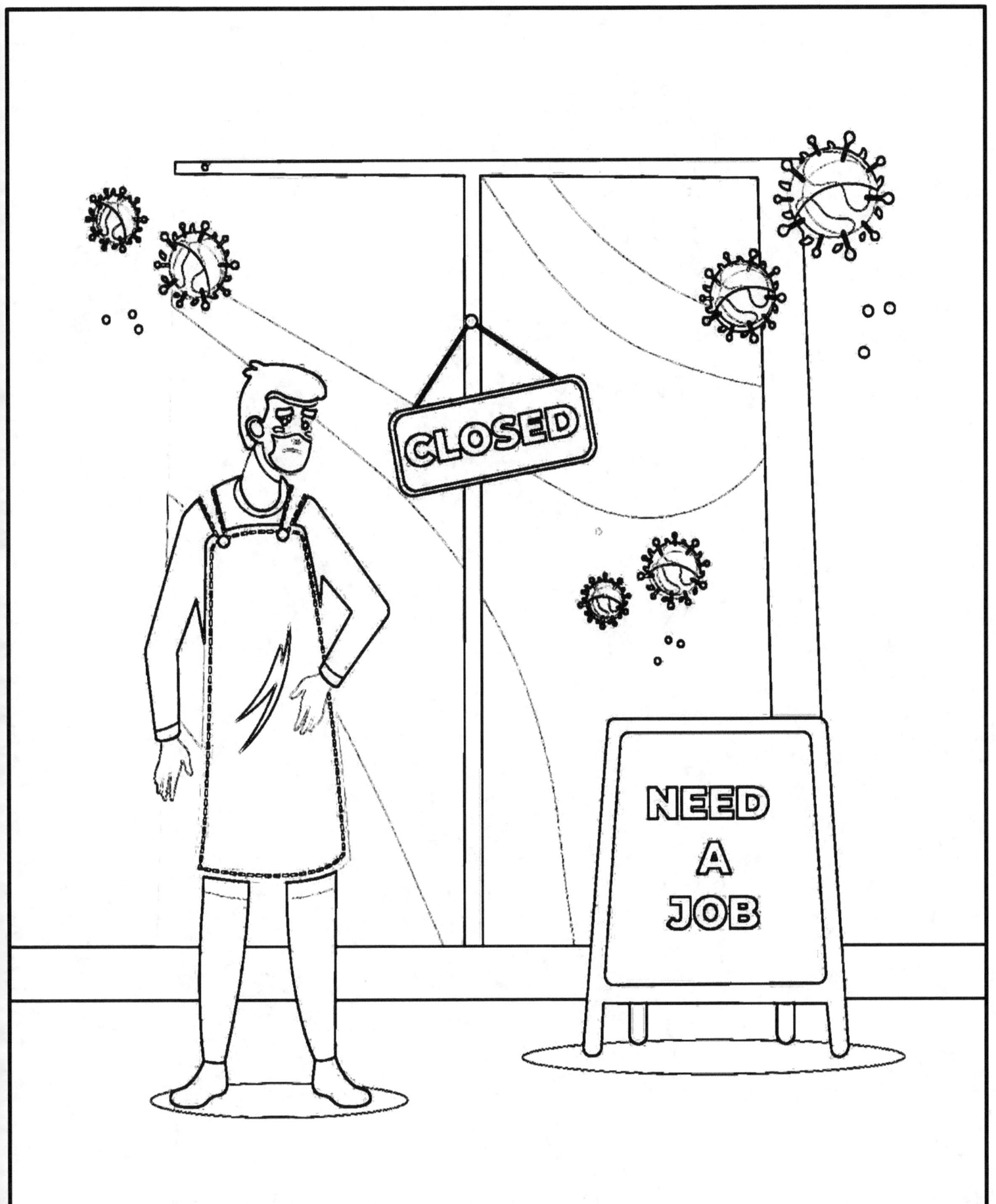

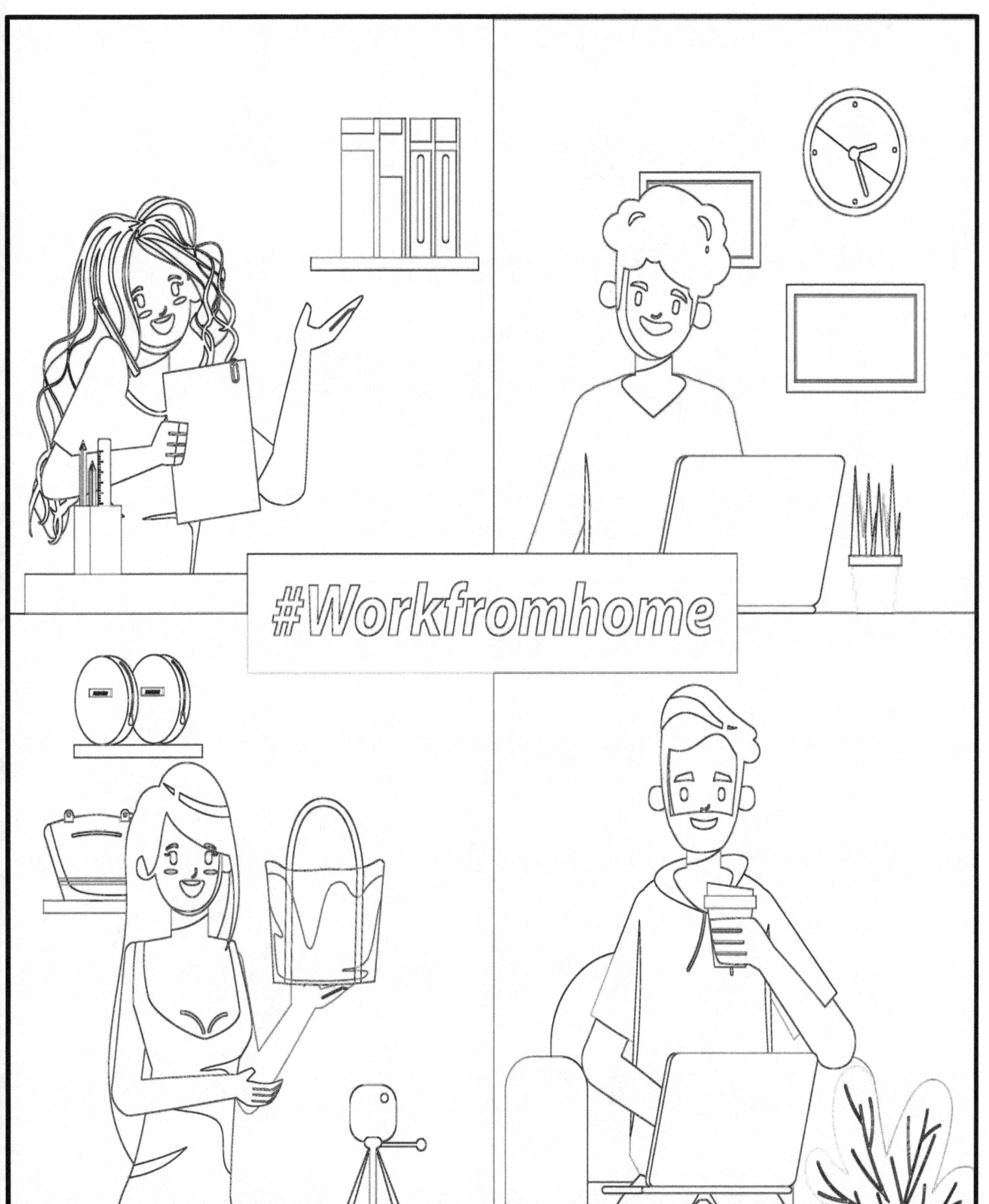

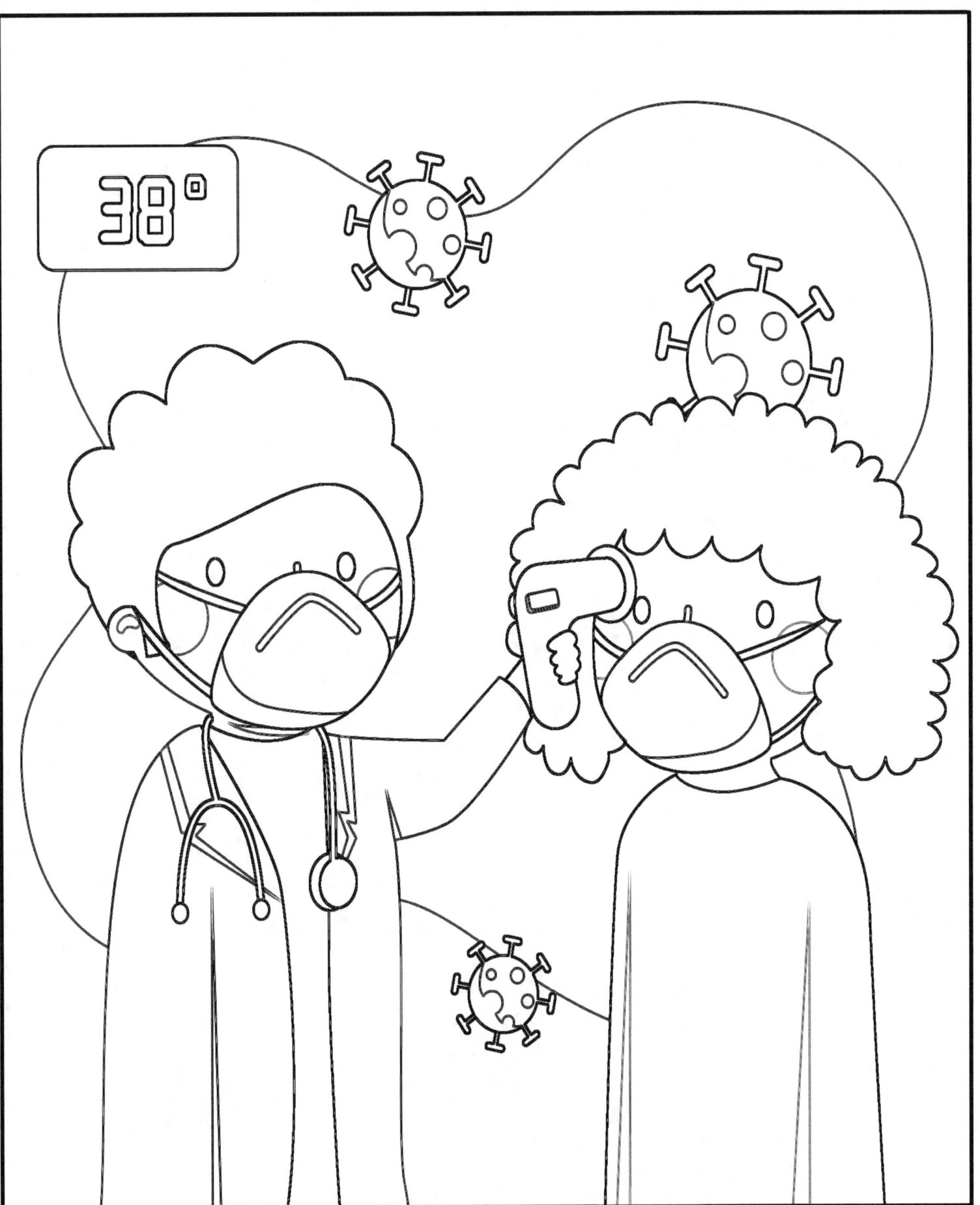

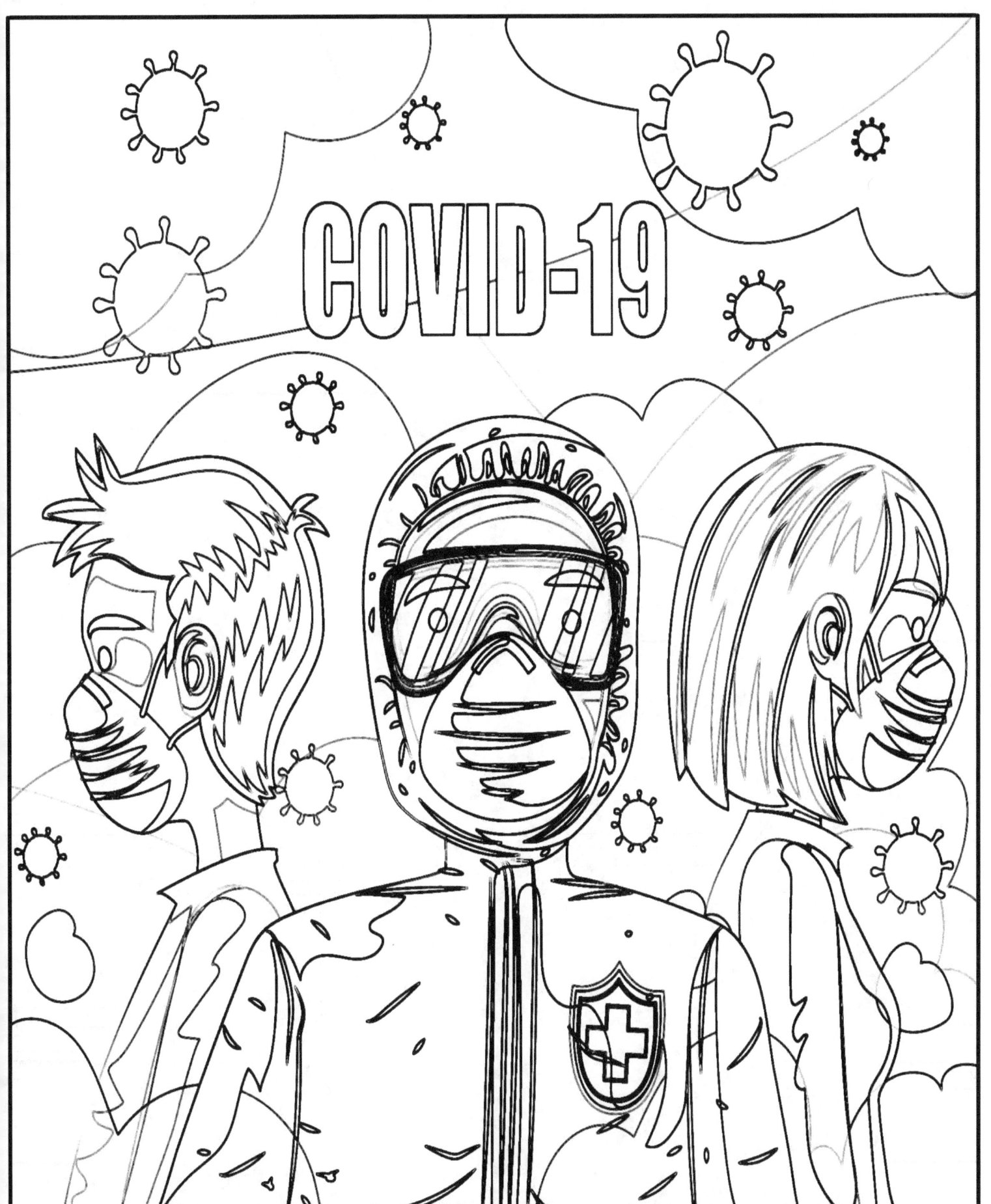

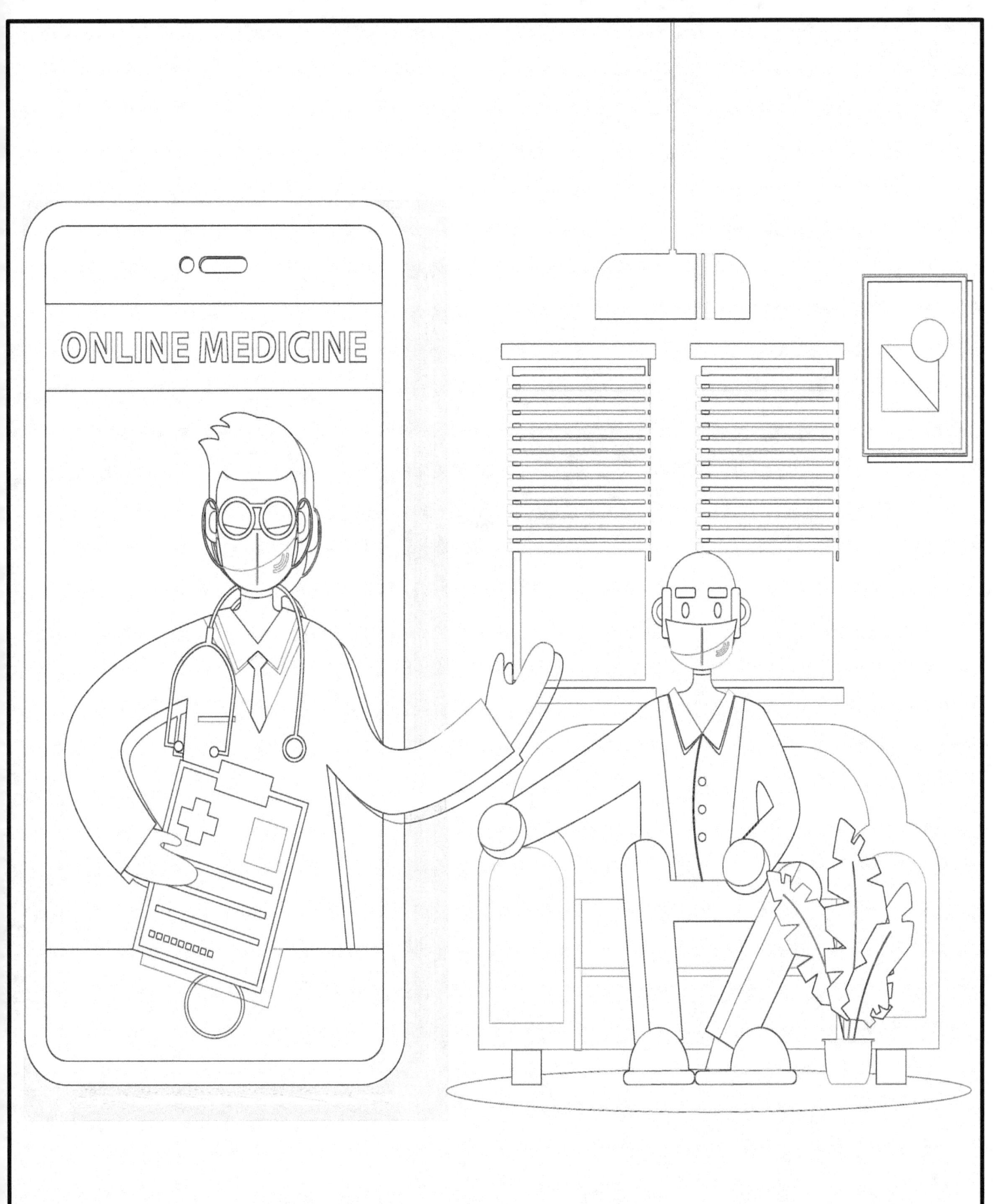

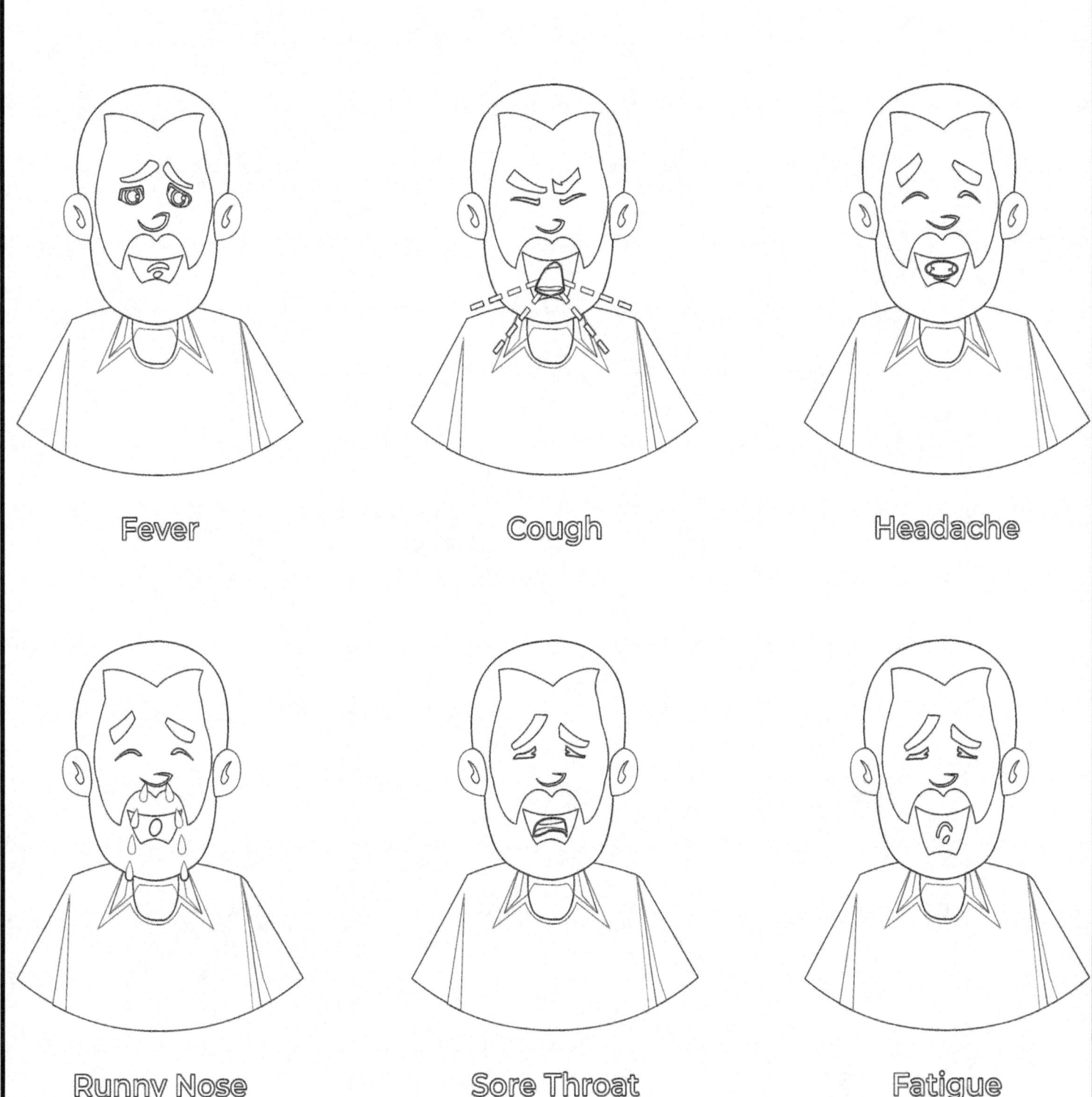

CORONAVIRUS PREVENTION

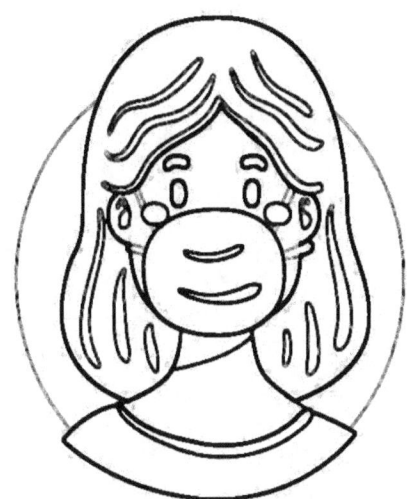
Wear mask

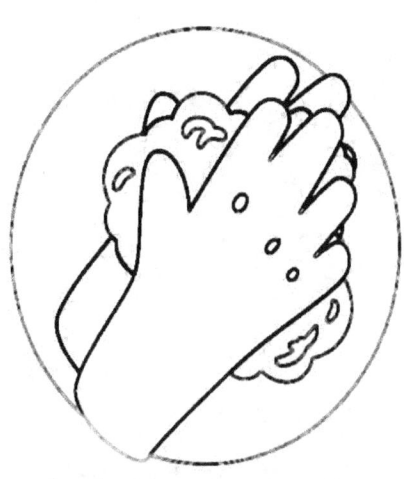
Wash hands

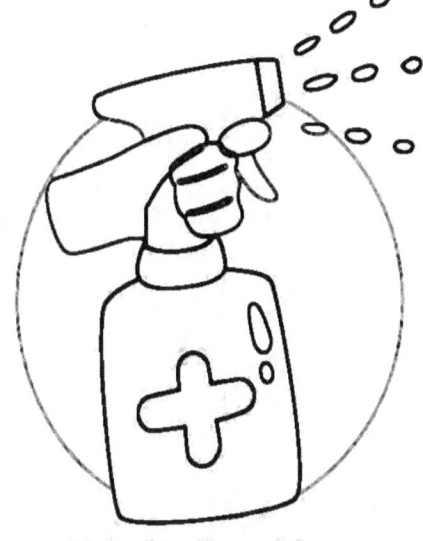
Disinfection

Avoid handshake

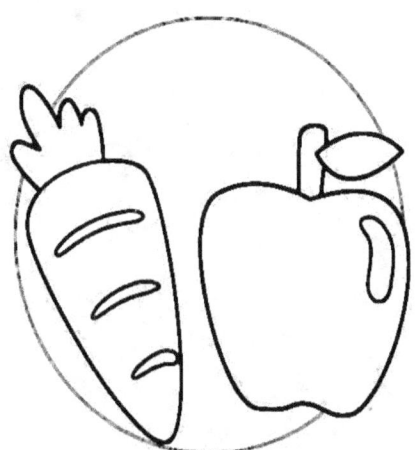
Eat fruit and vegetable

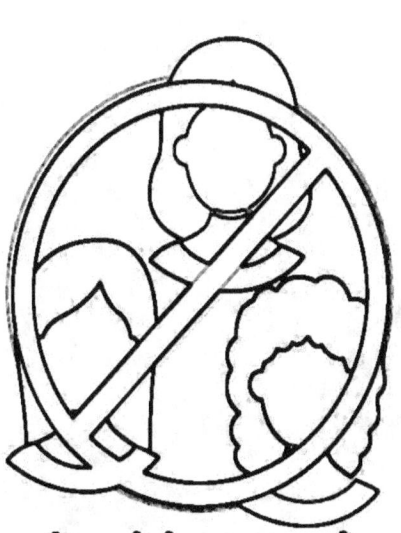
Avoid crowds

Disinfection

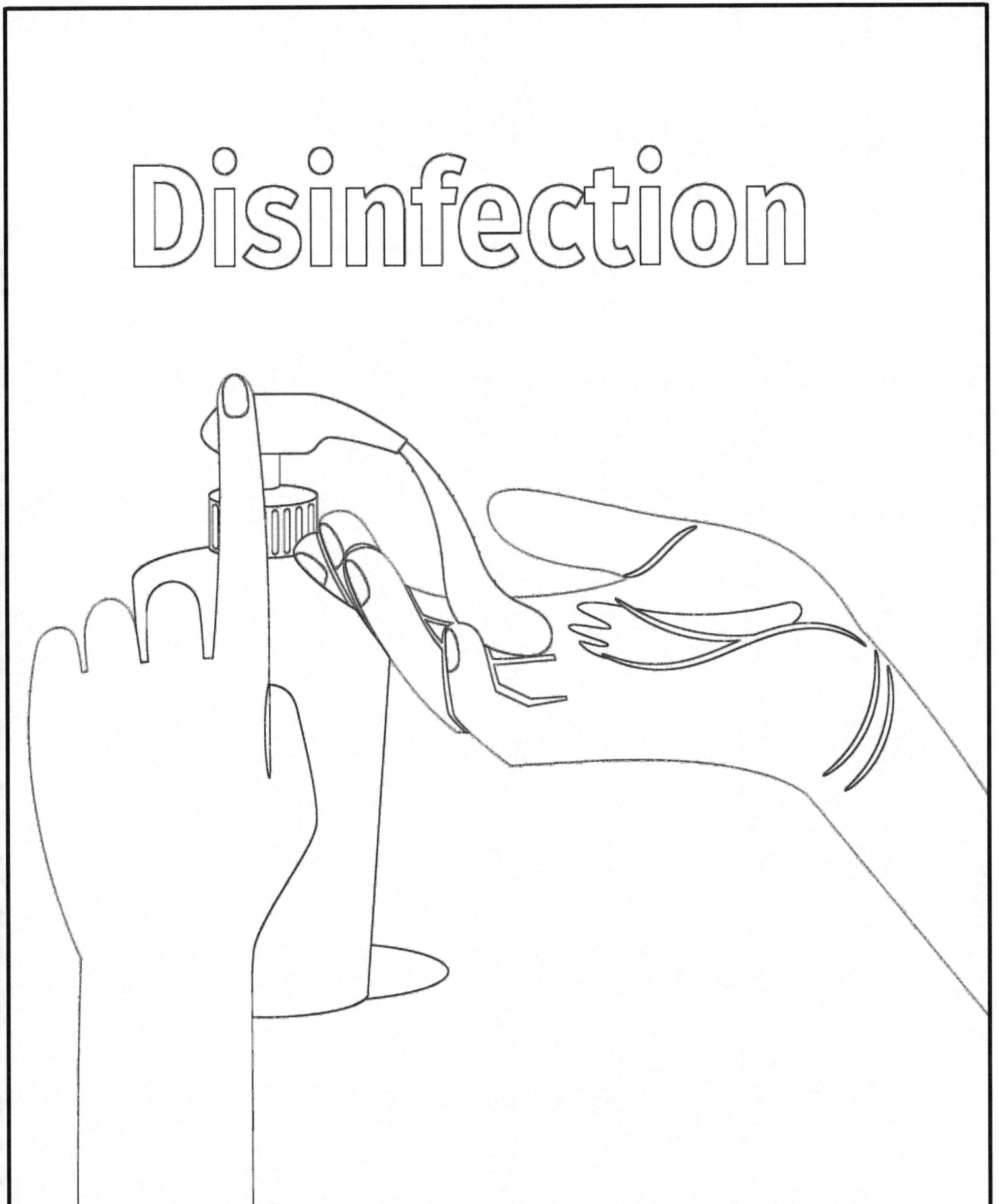

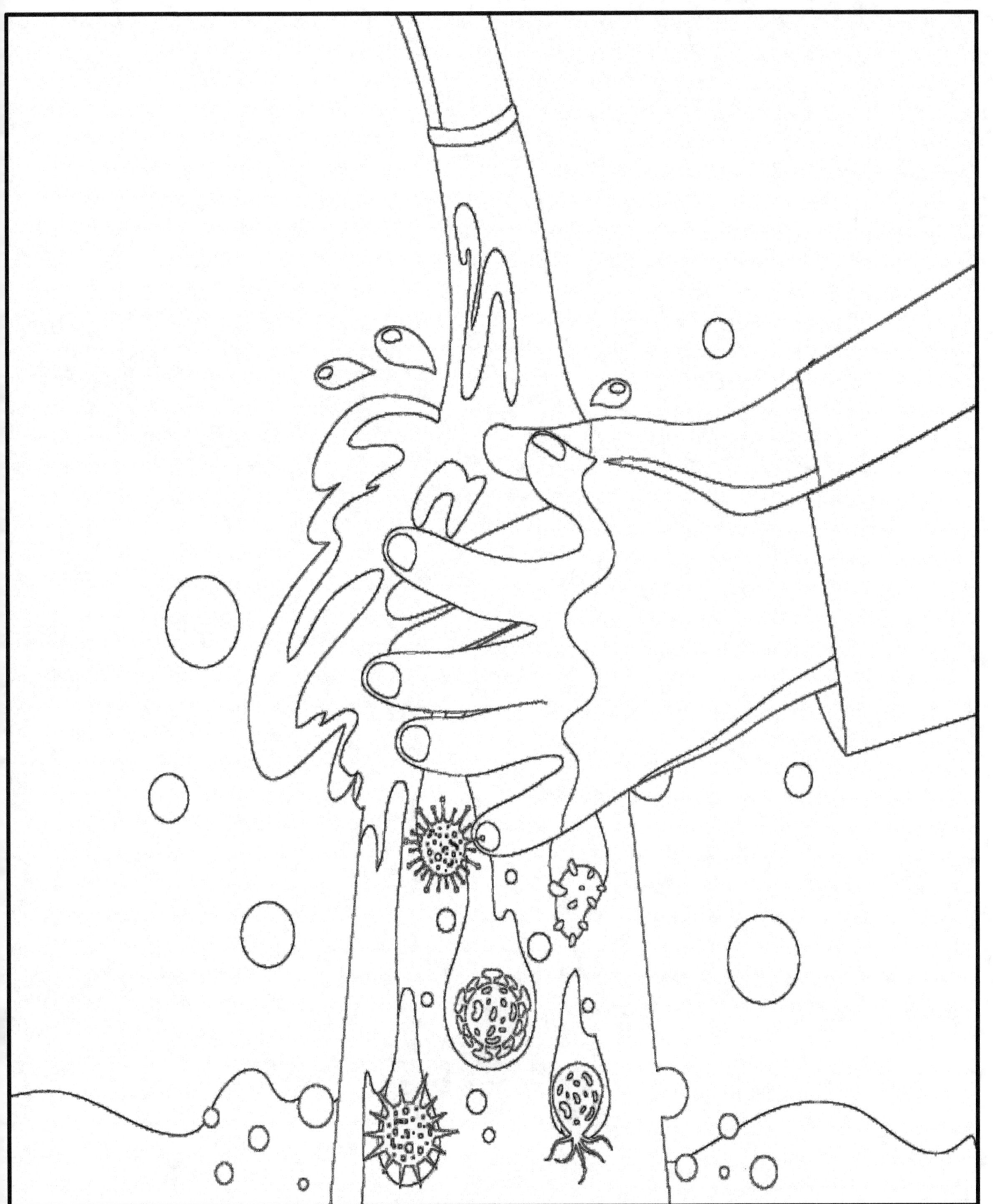

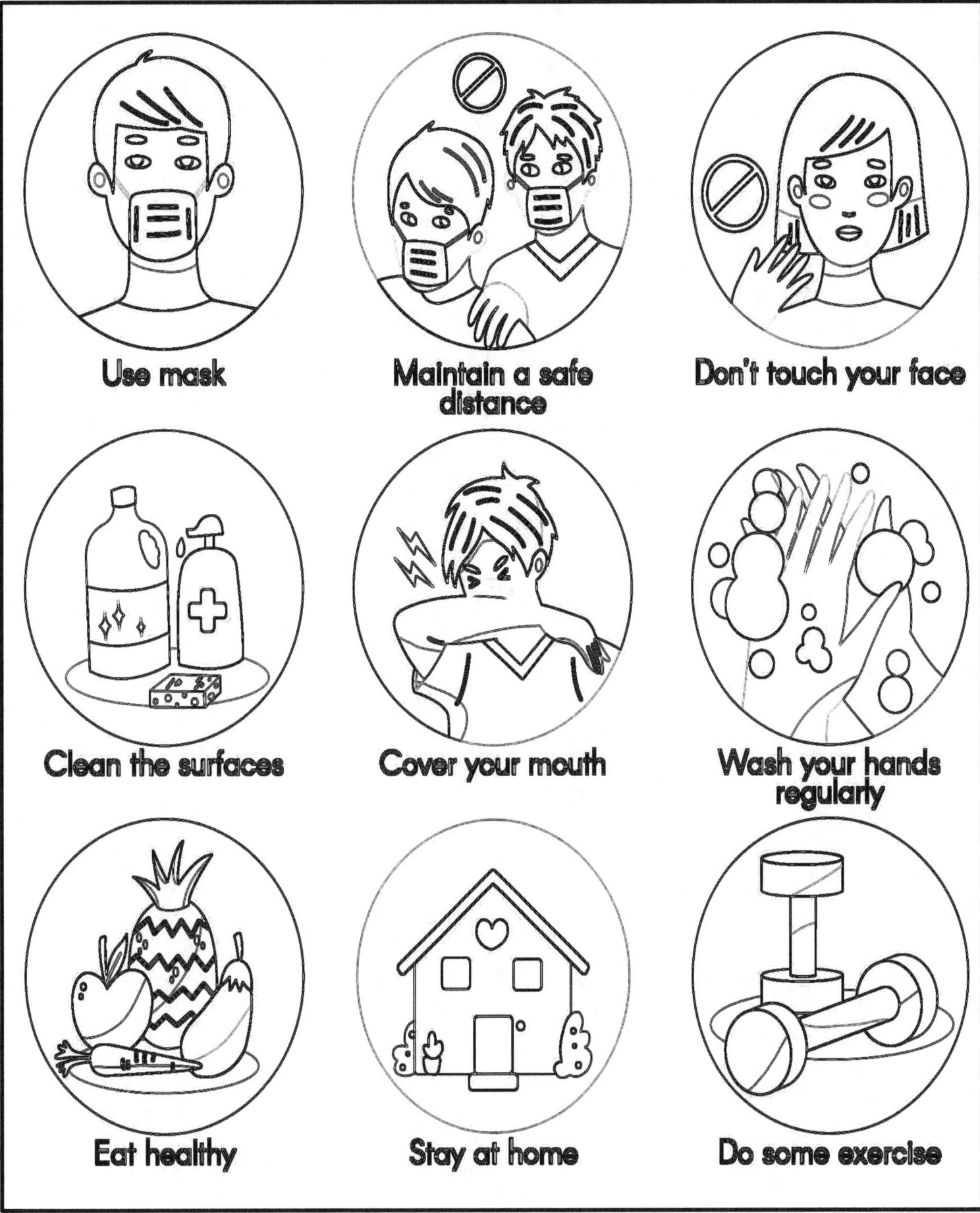

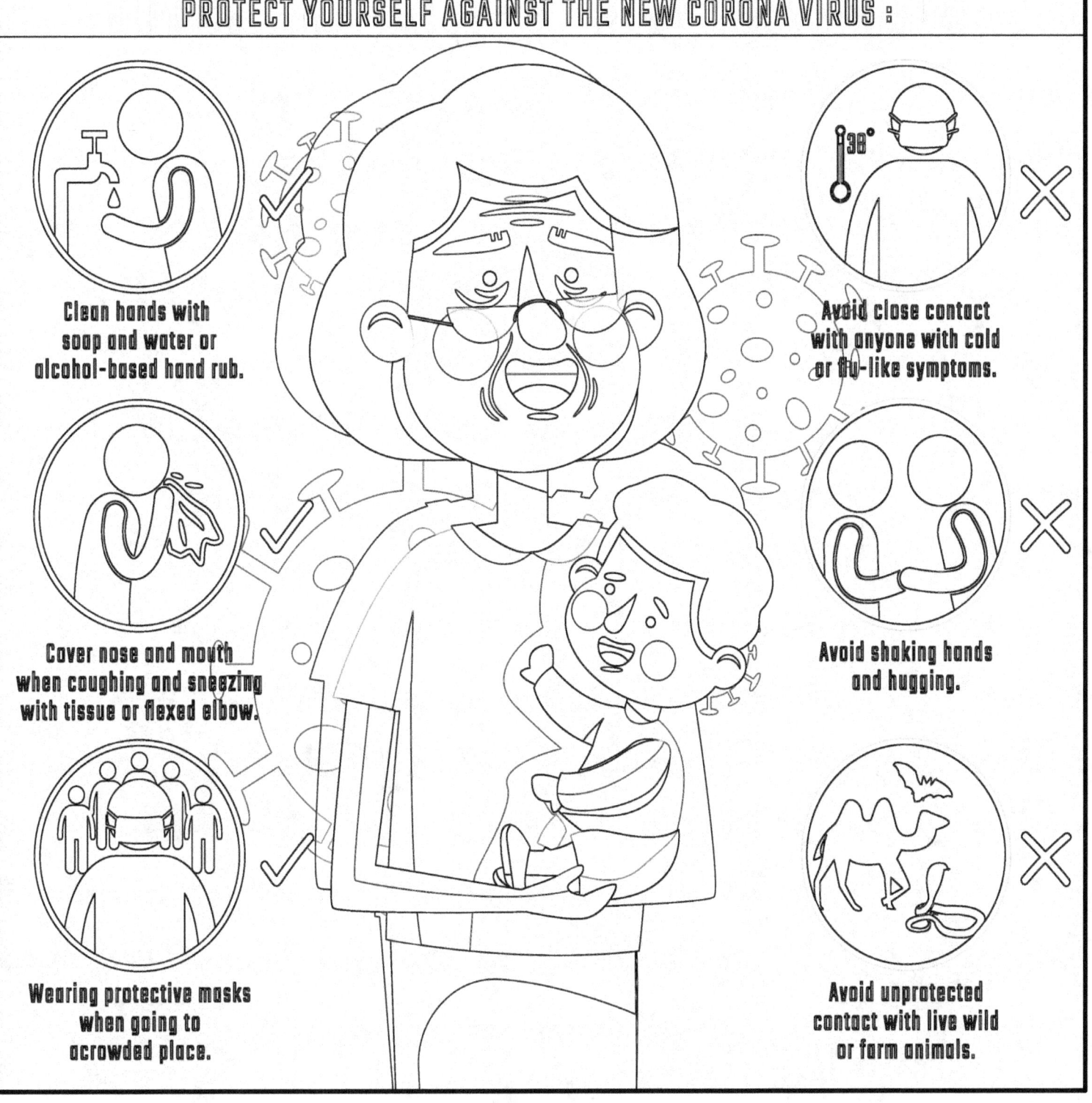

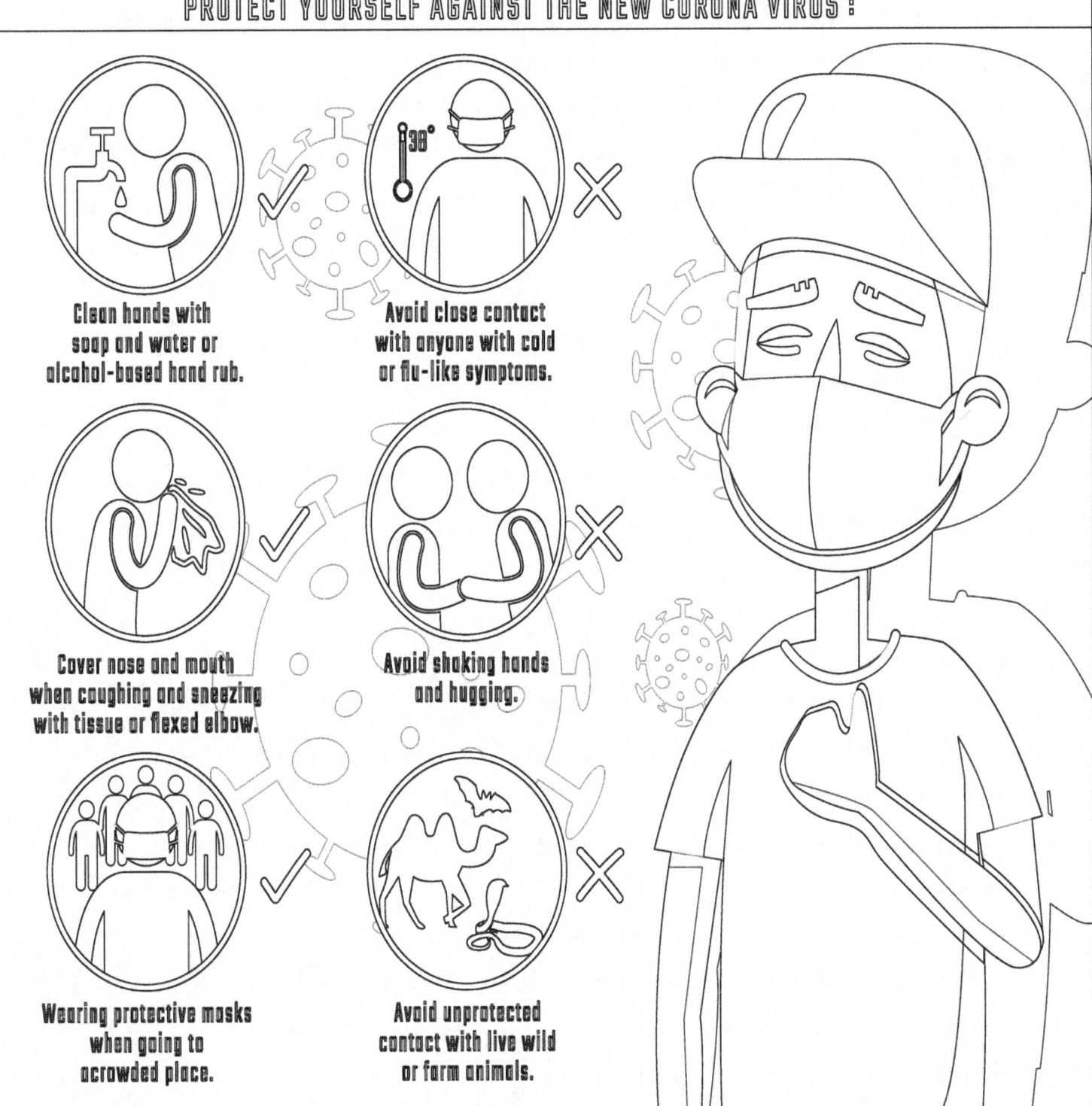

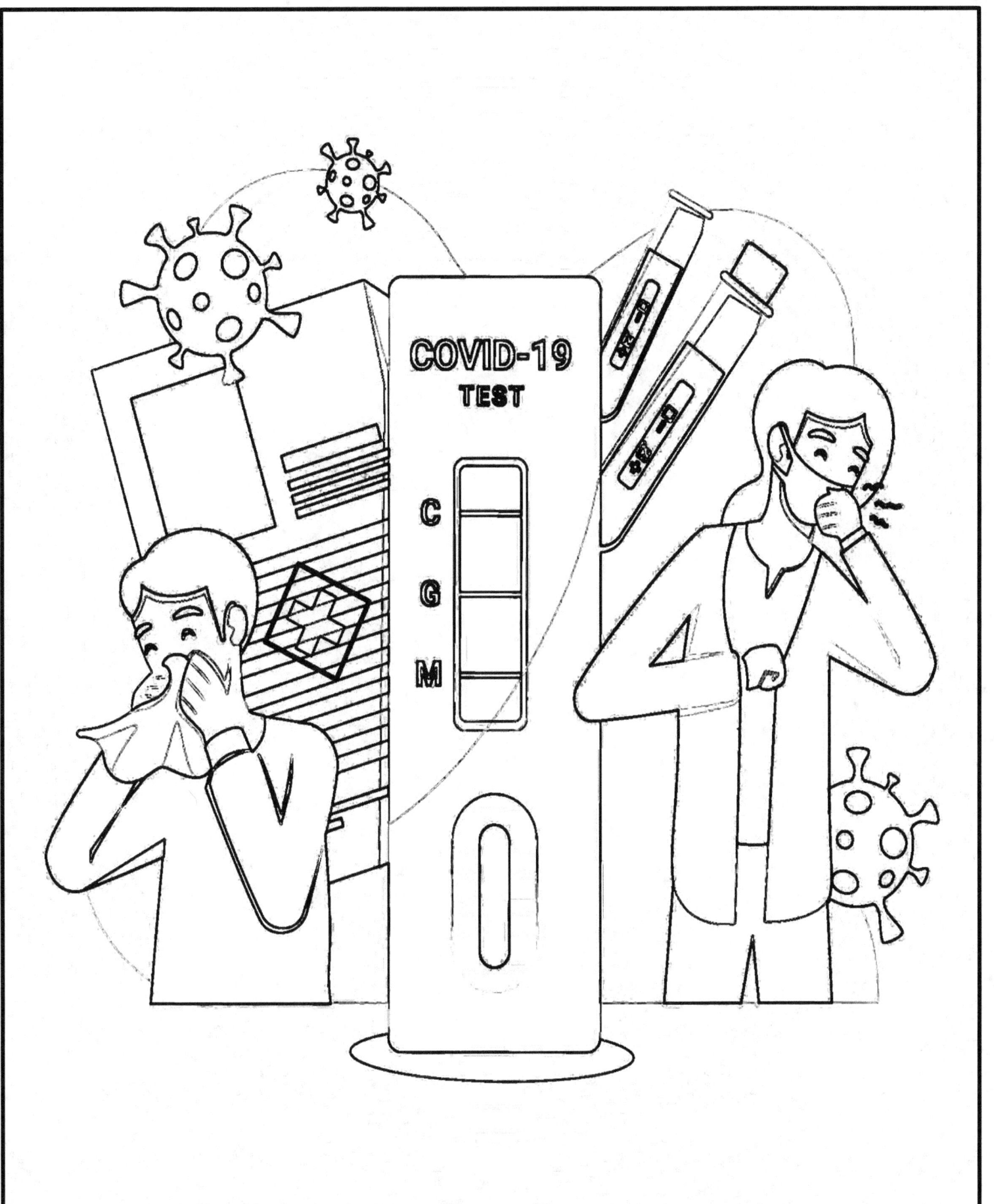

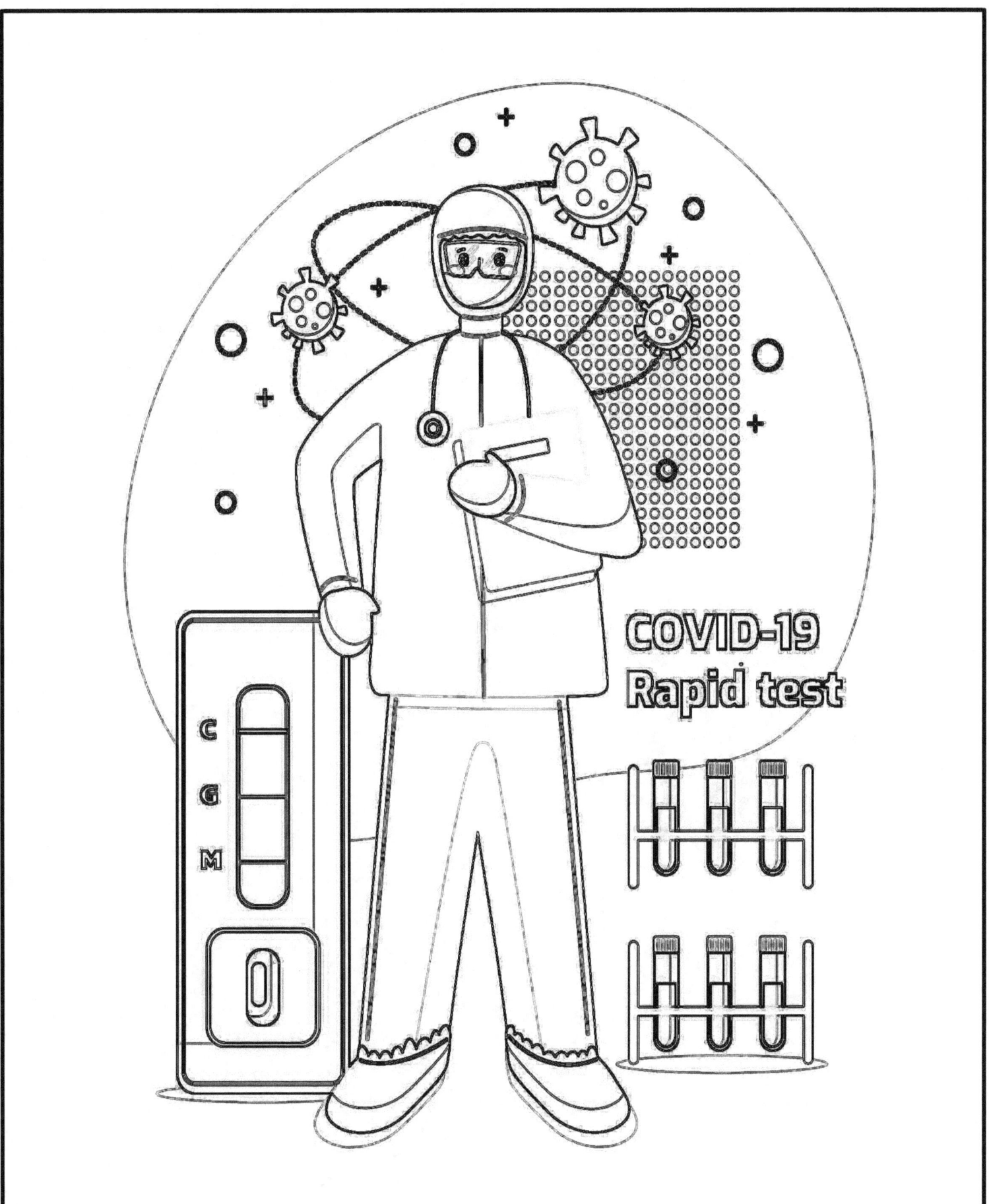

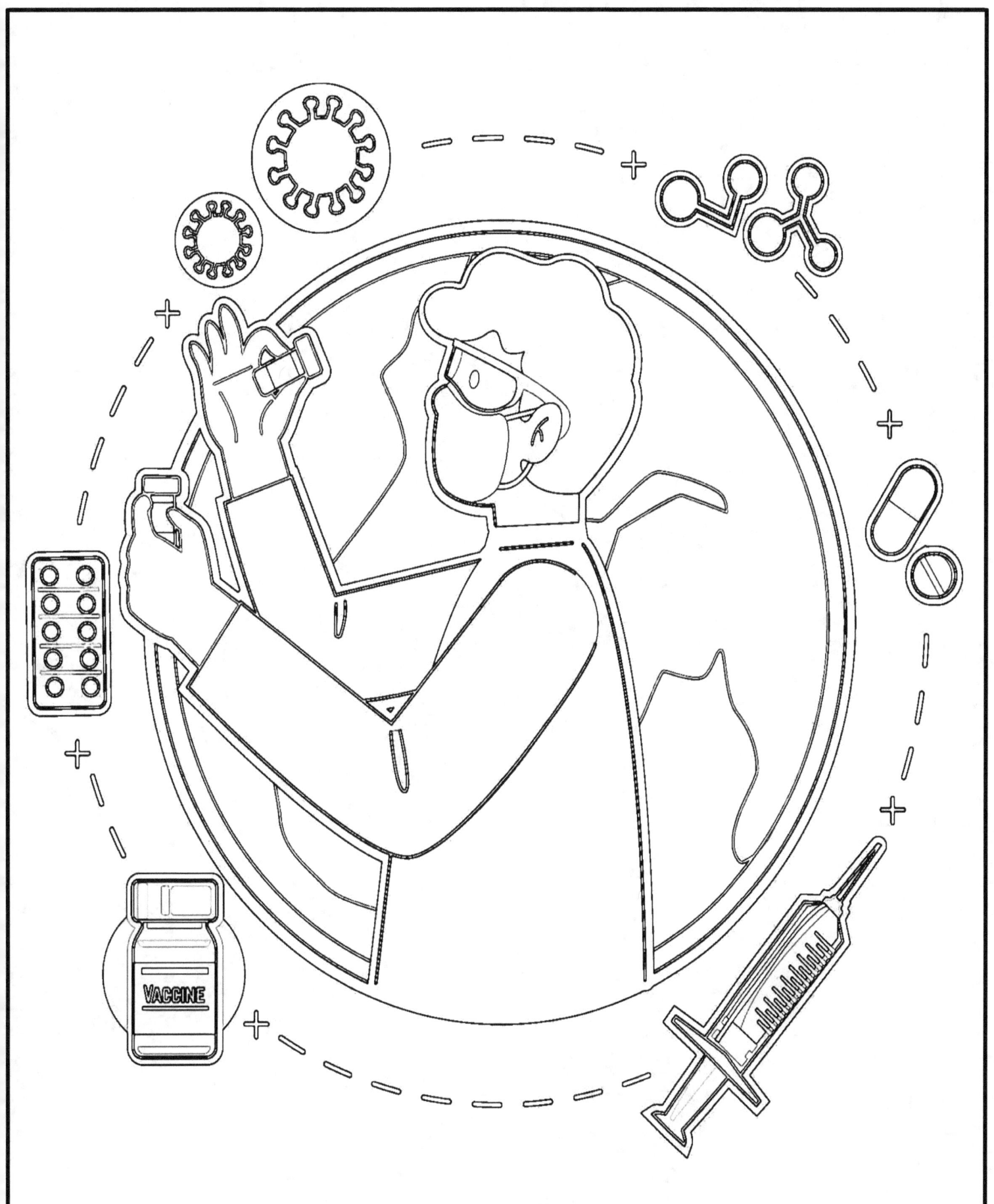

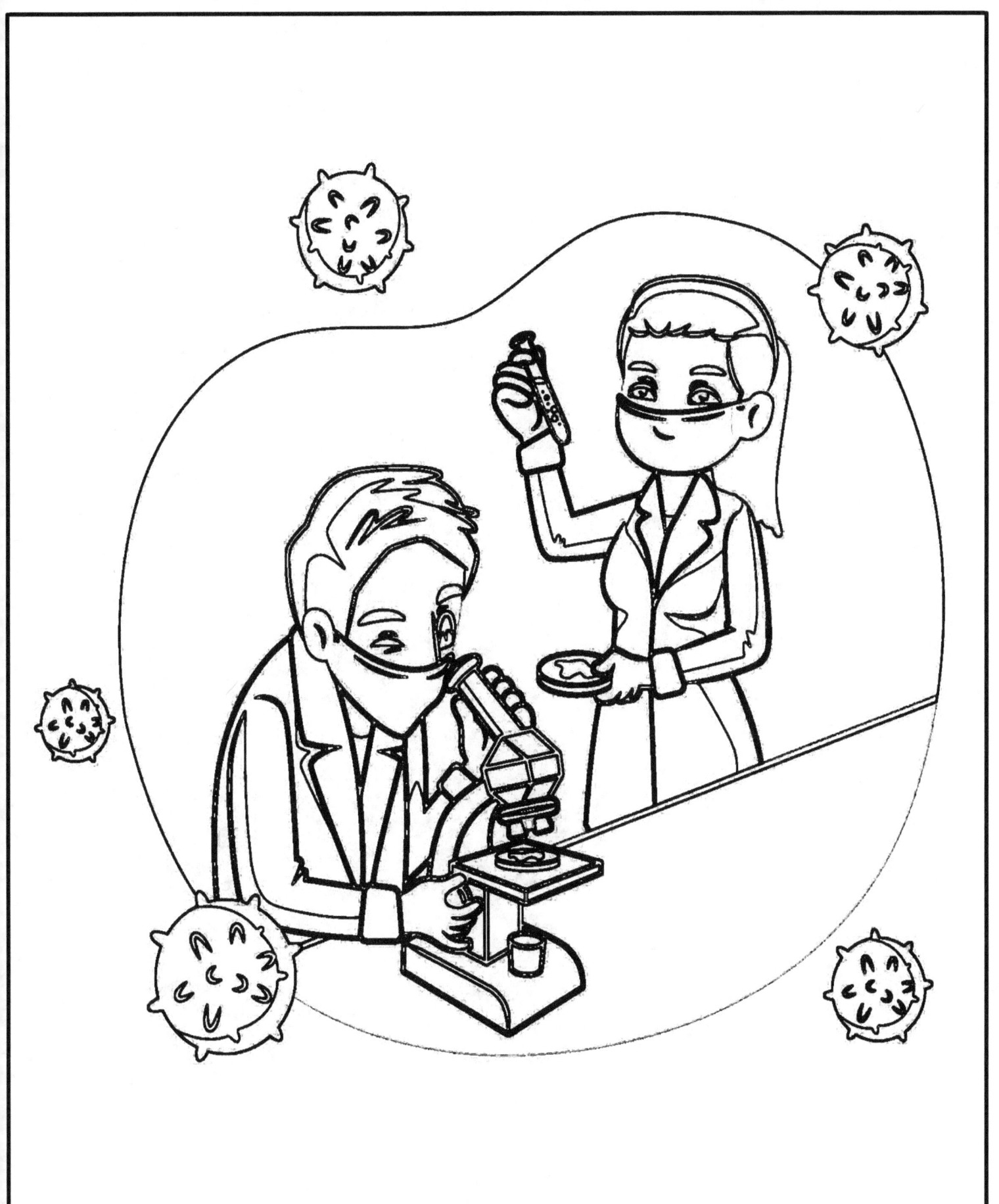

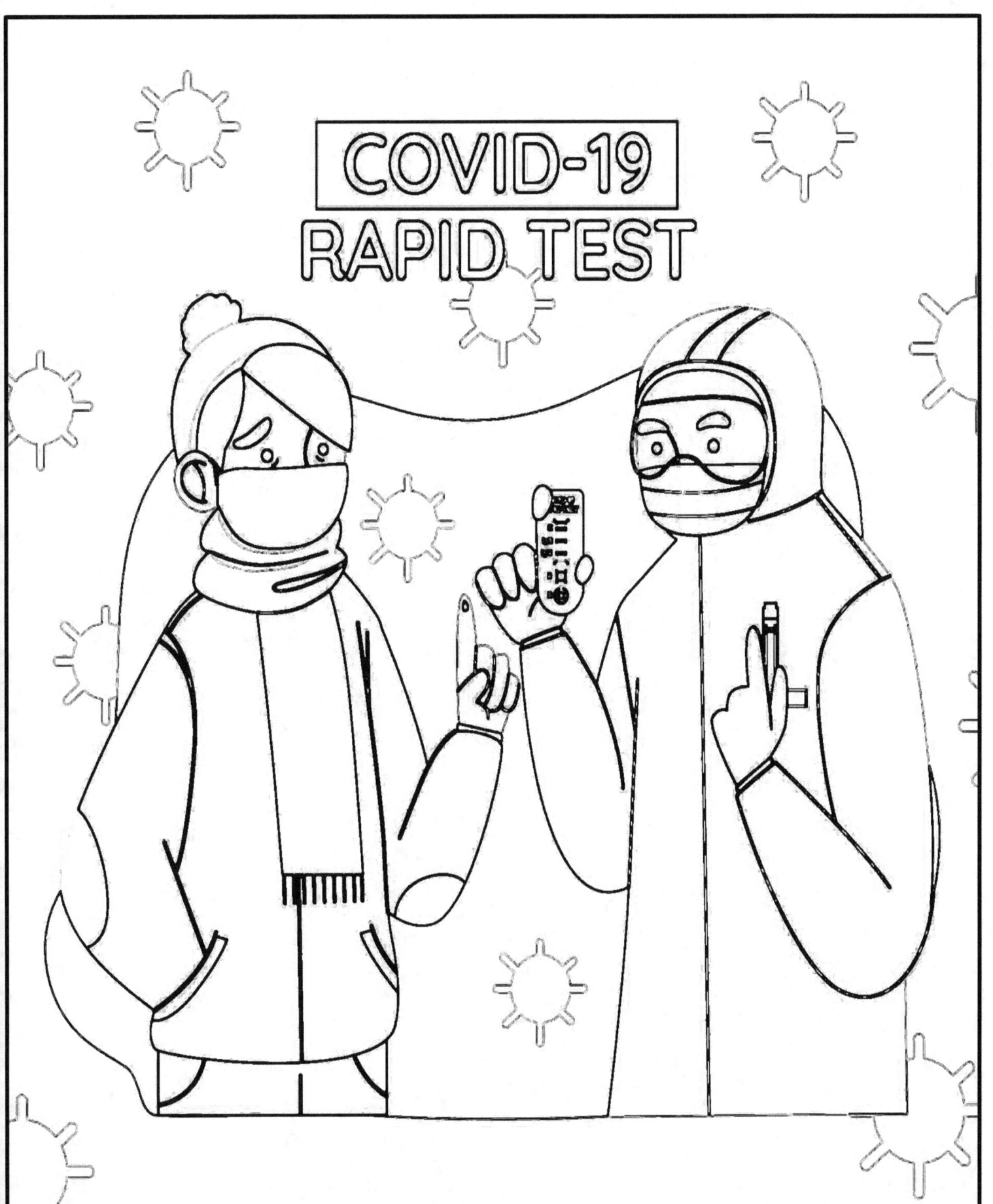

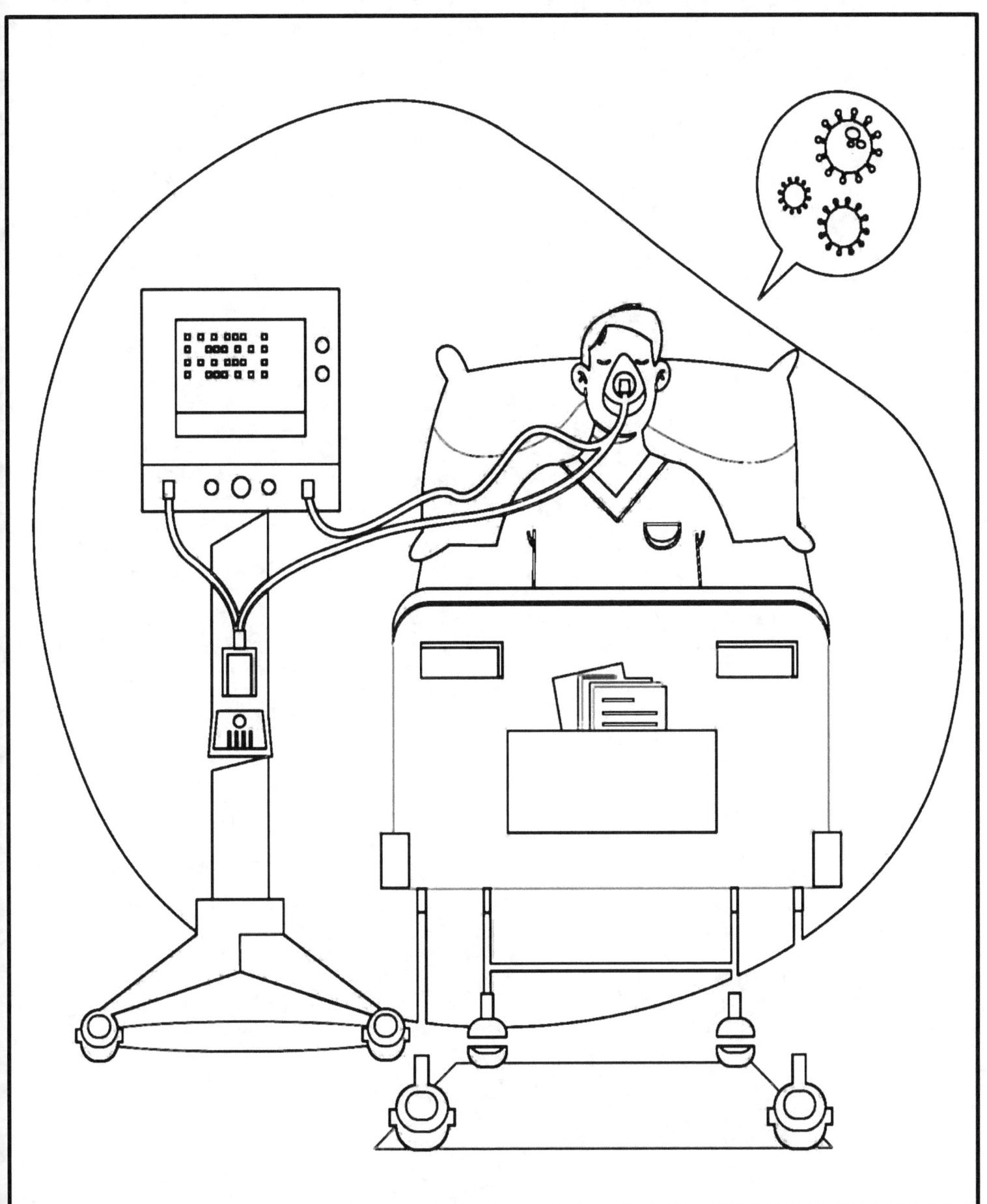

.45.

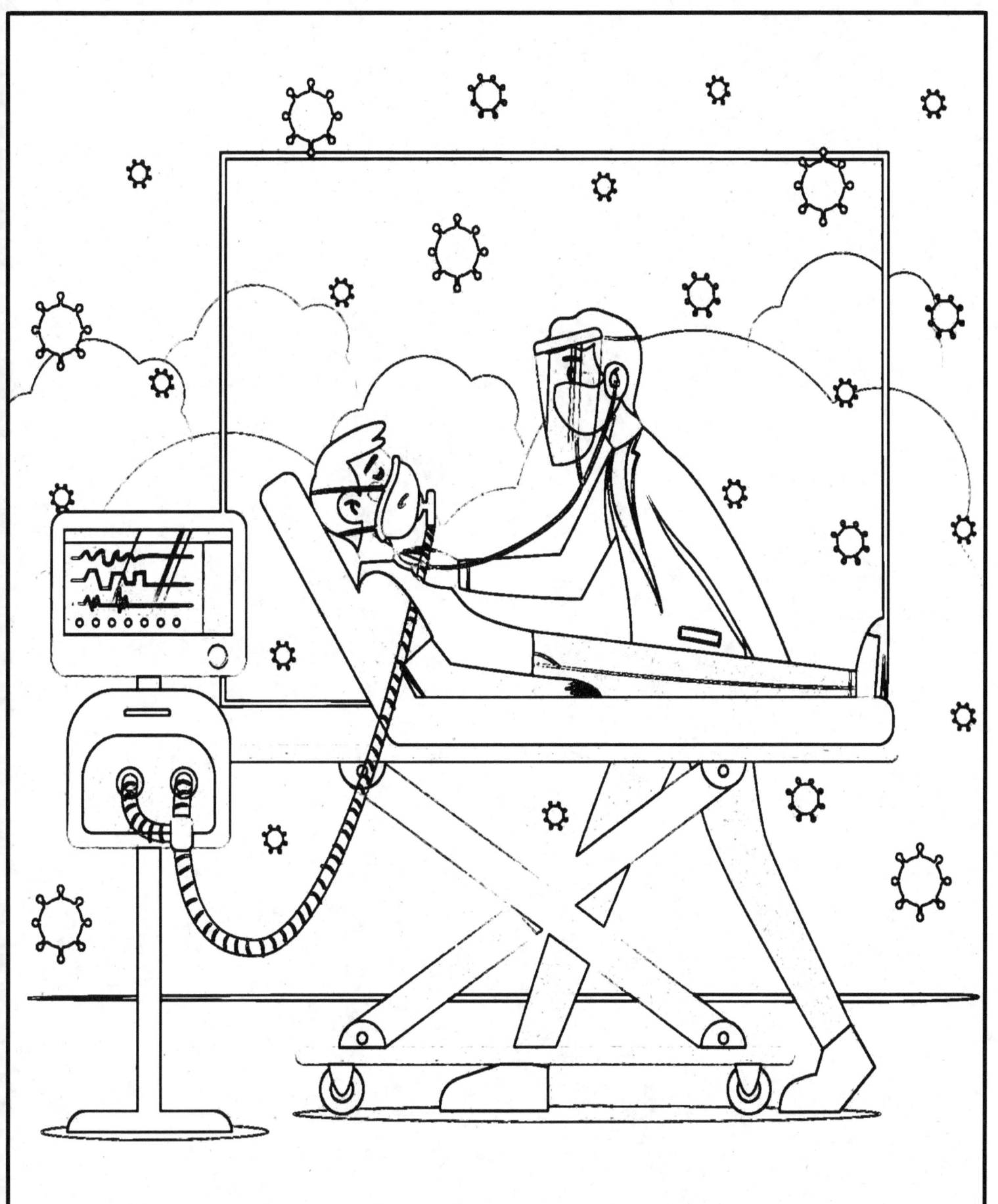

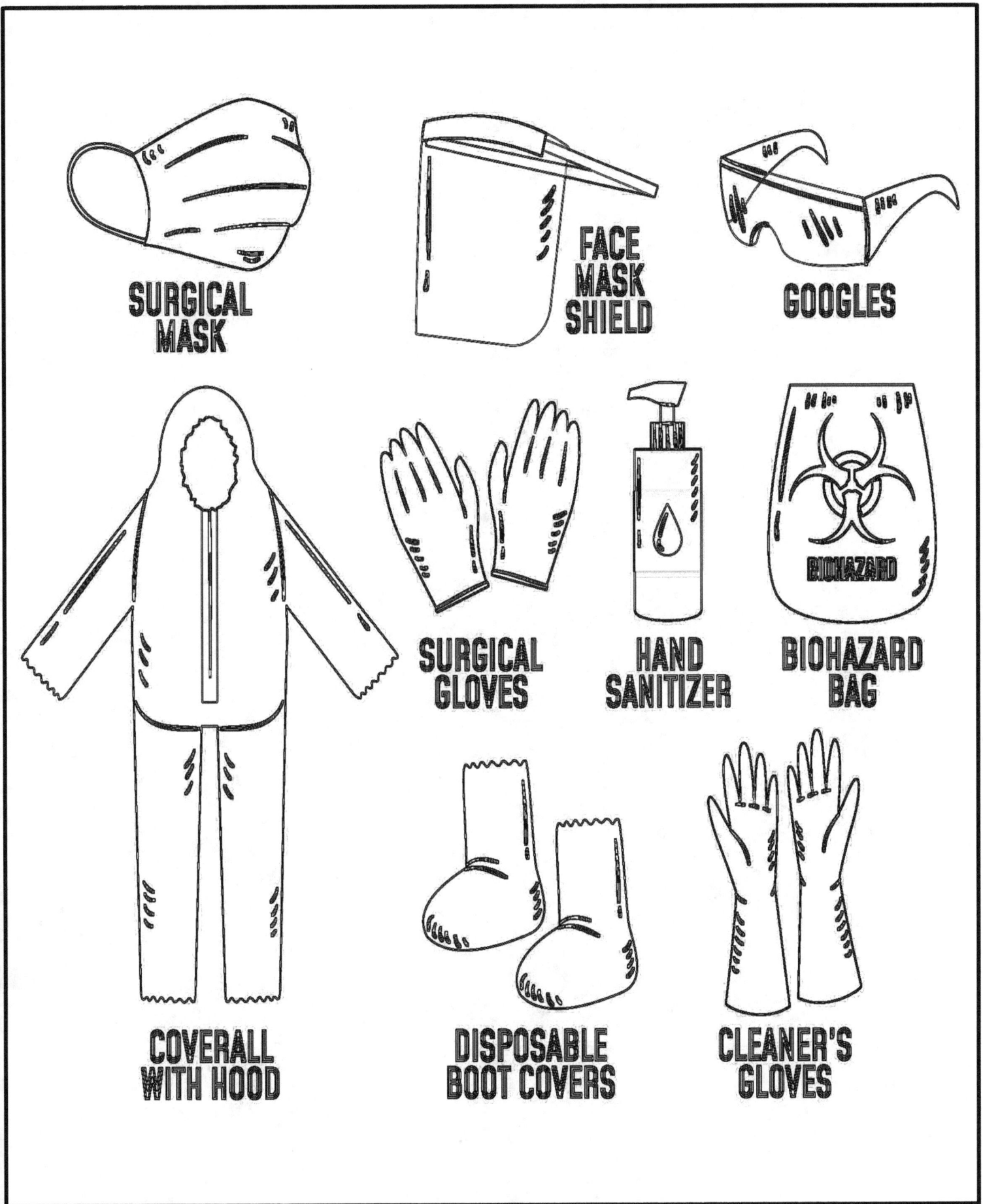

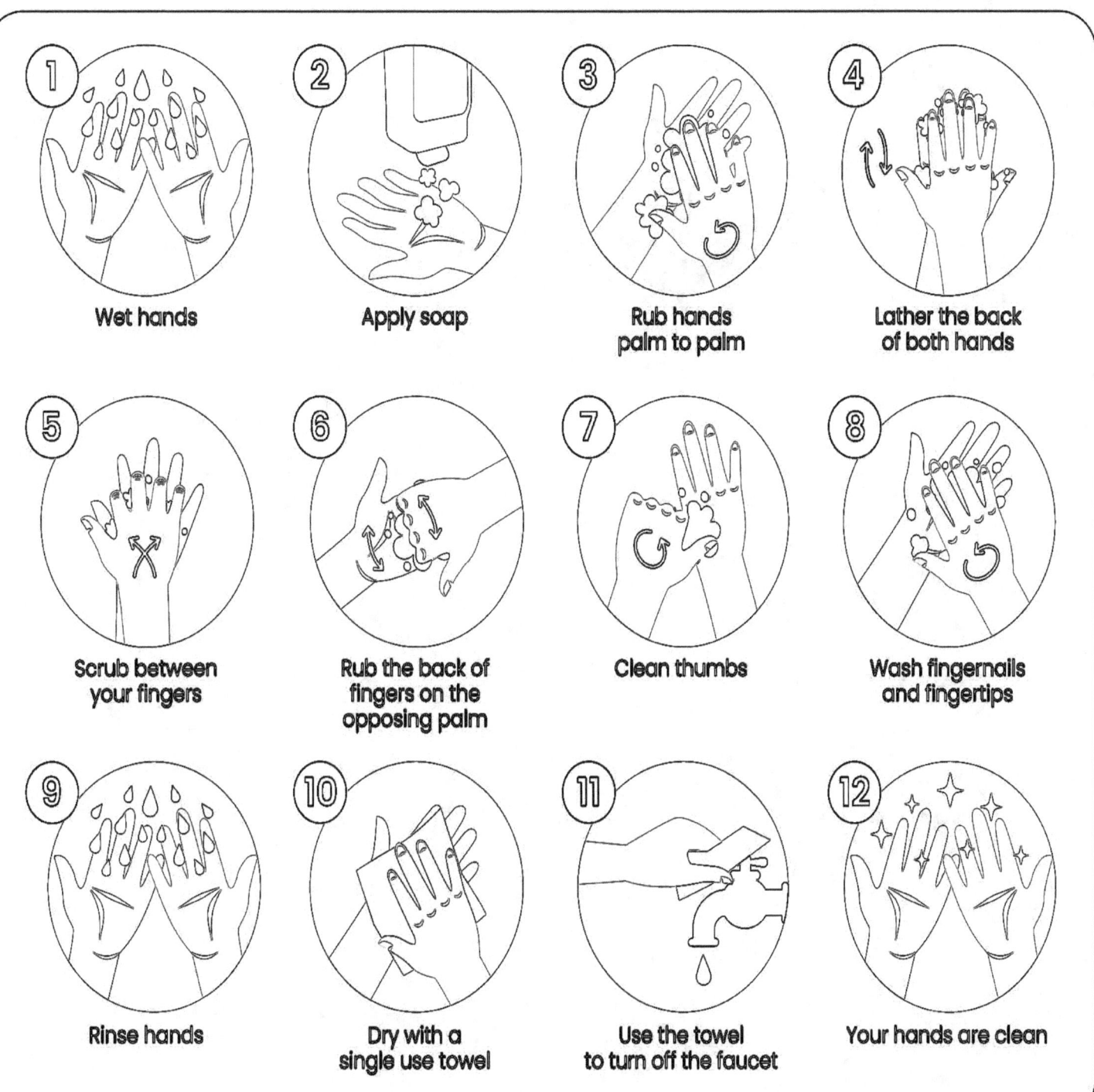

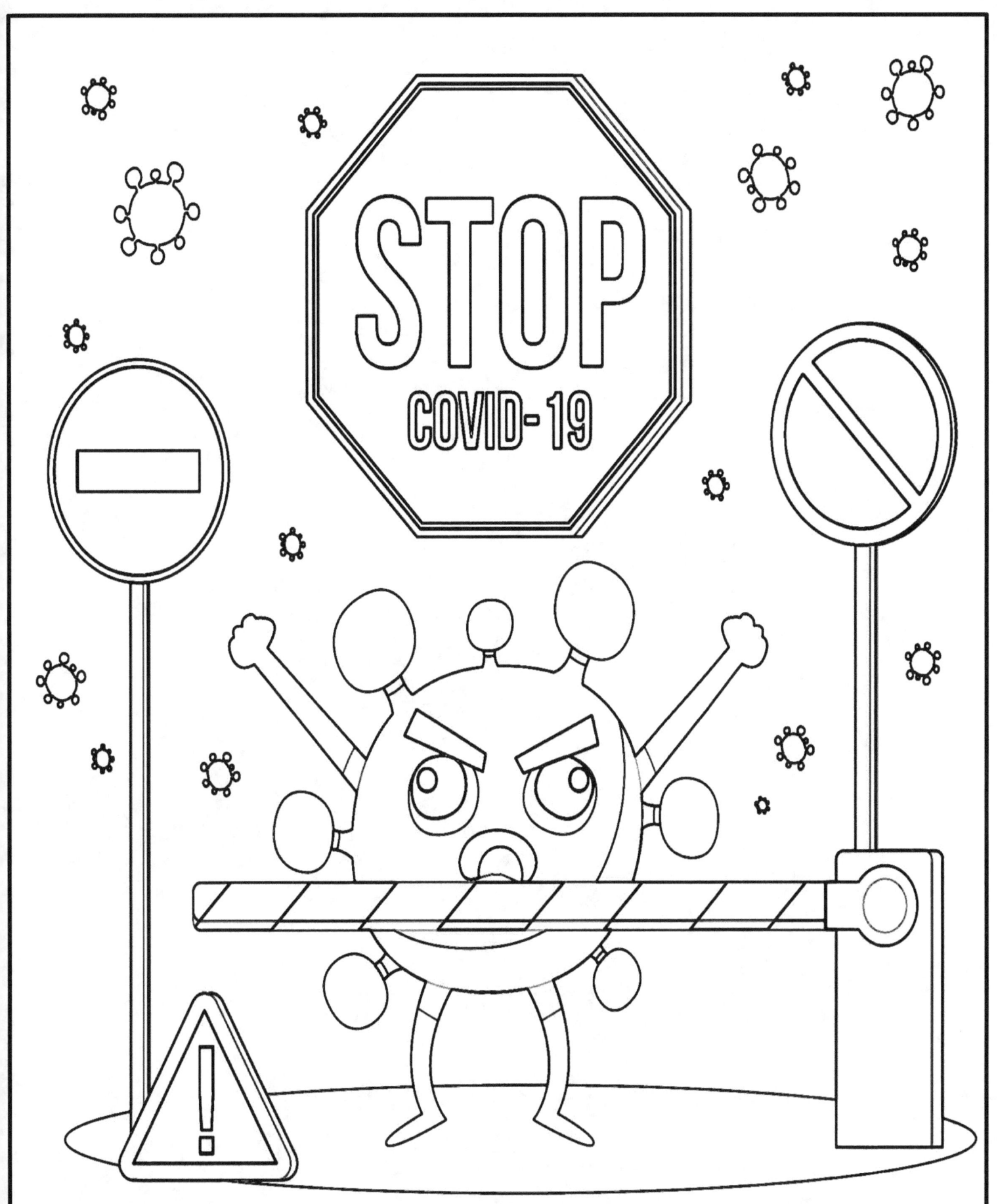

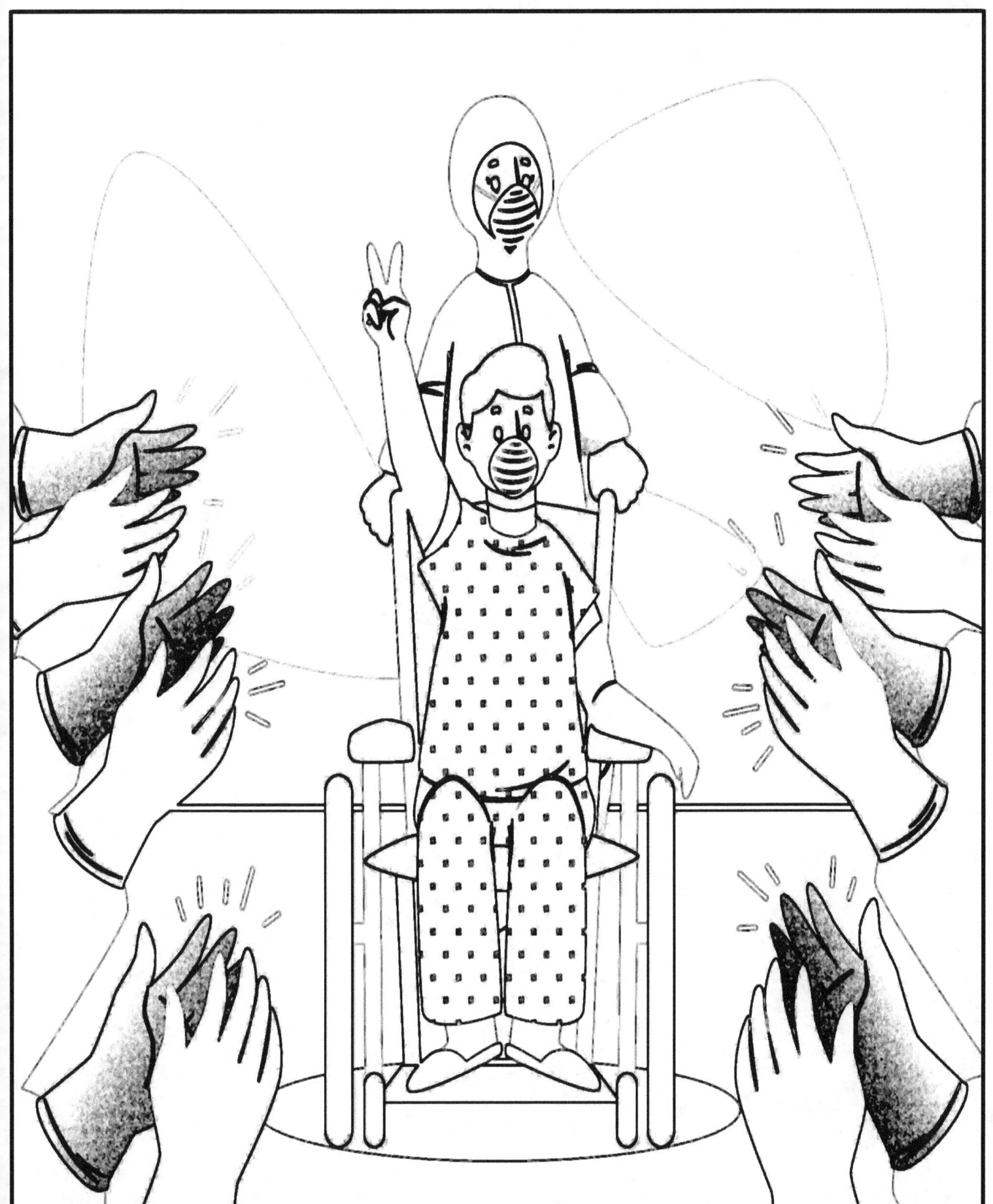

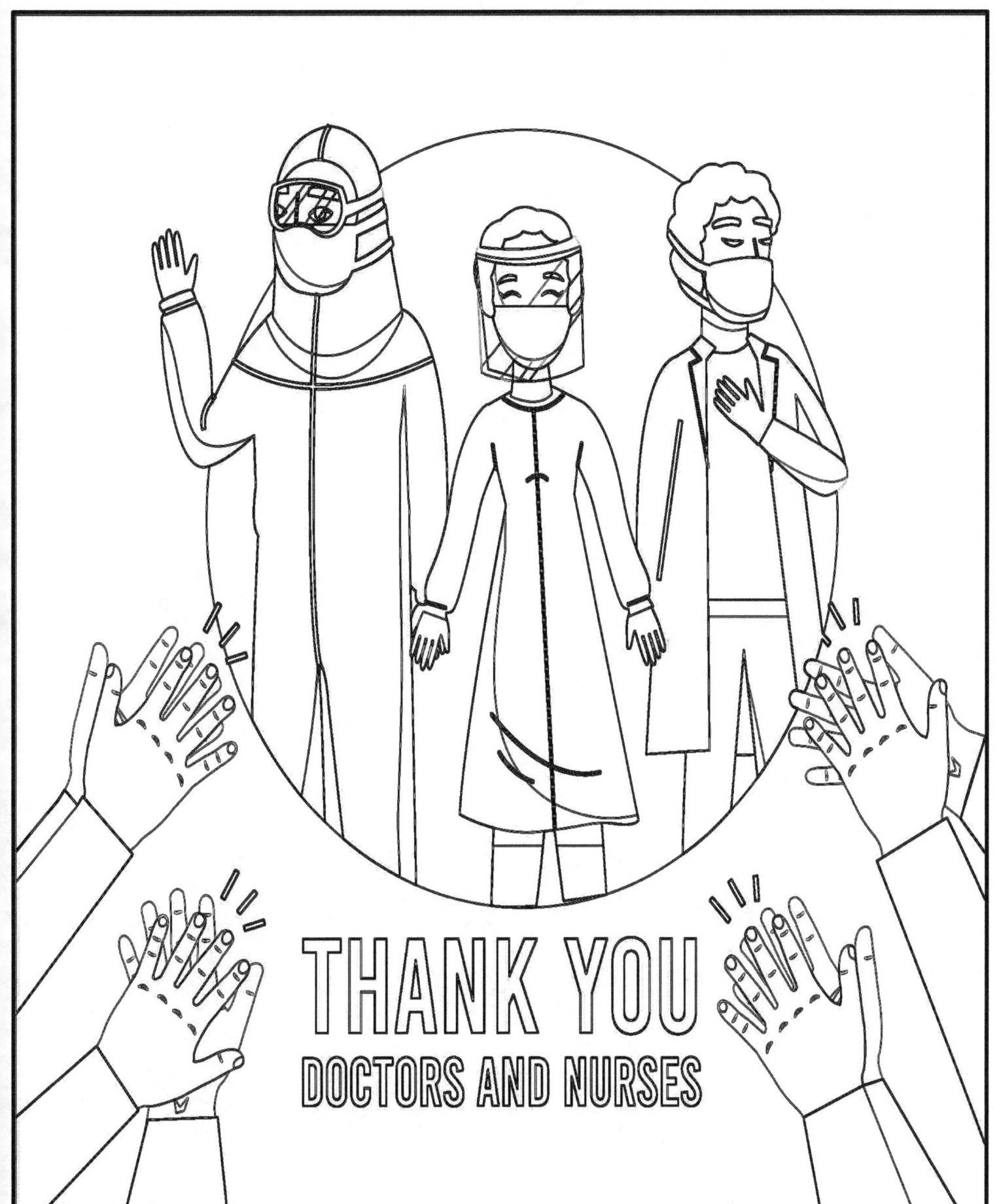

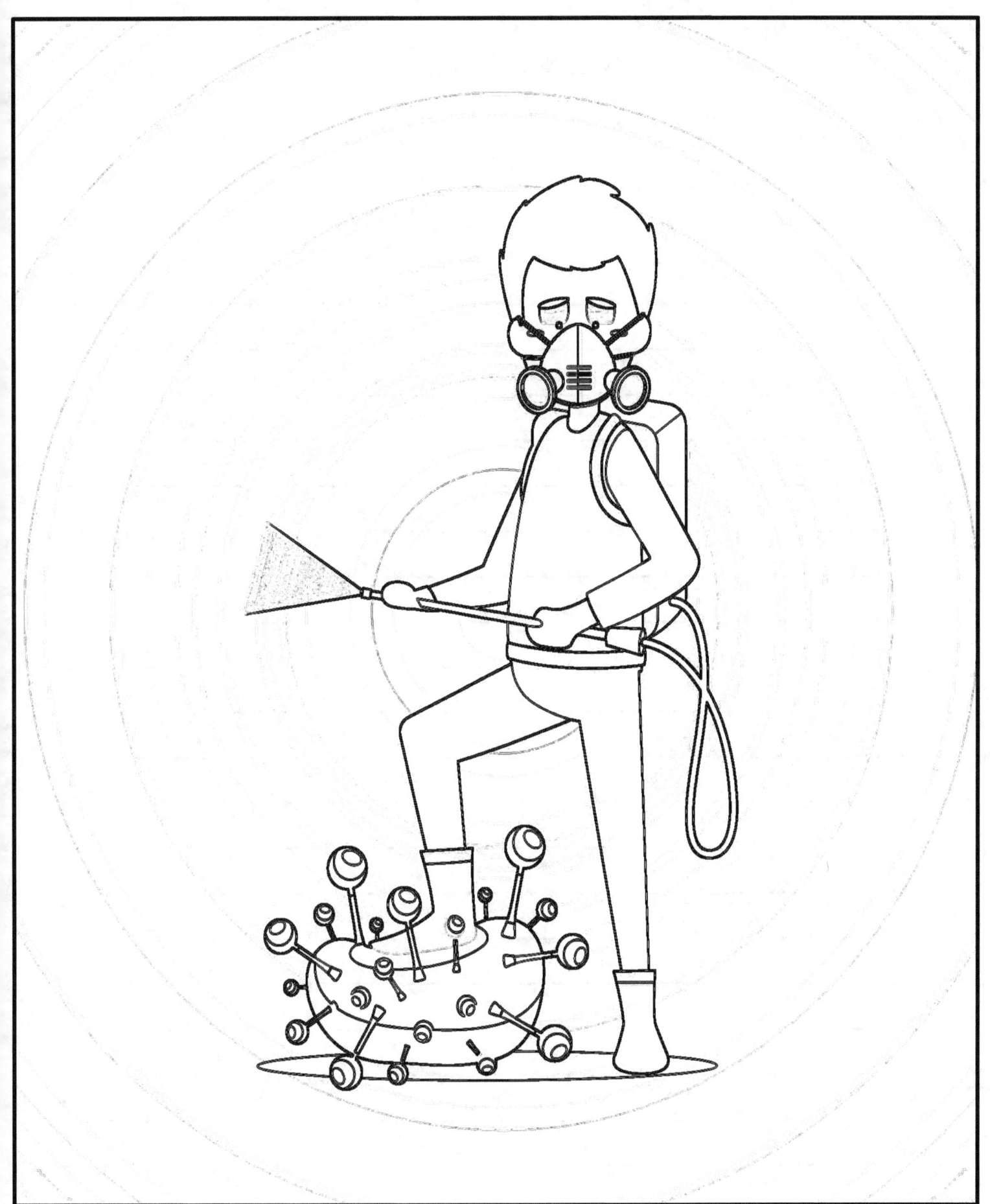

.52.

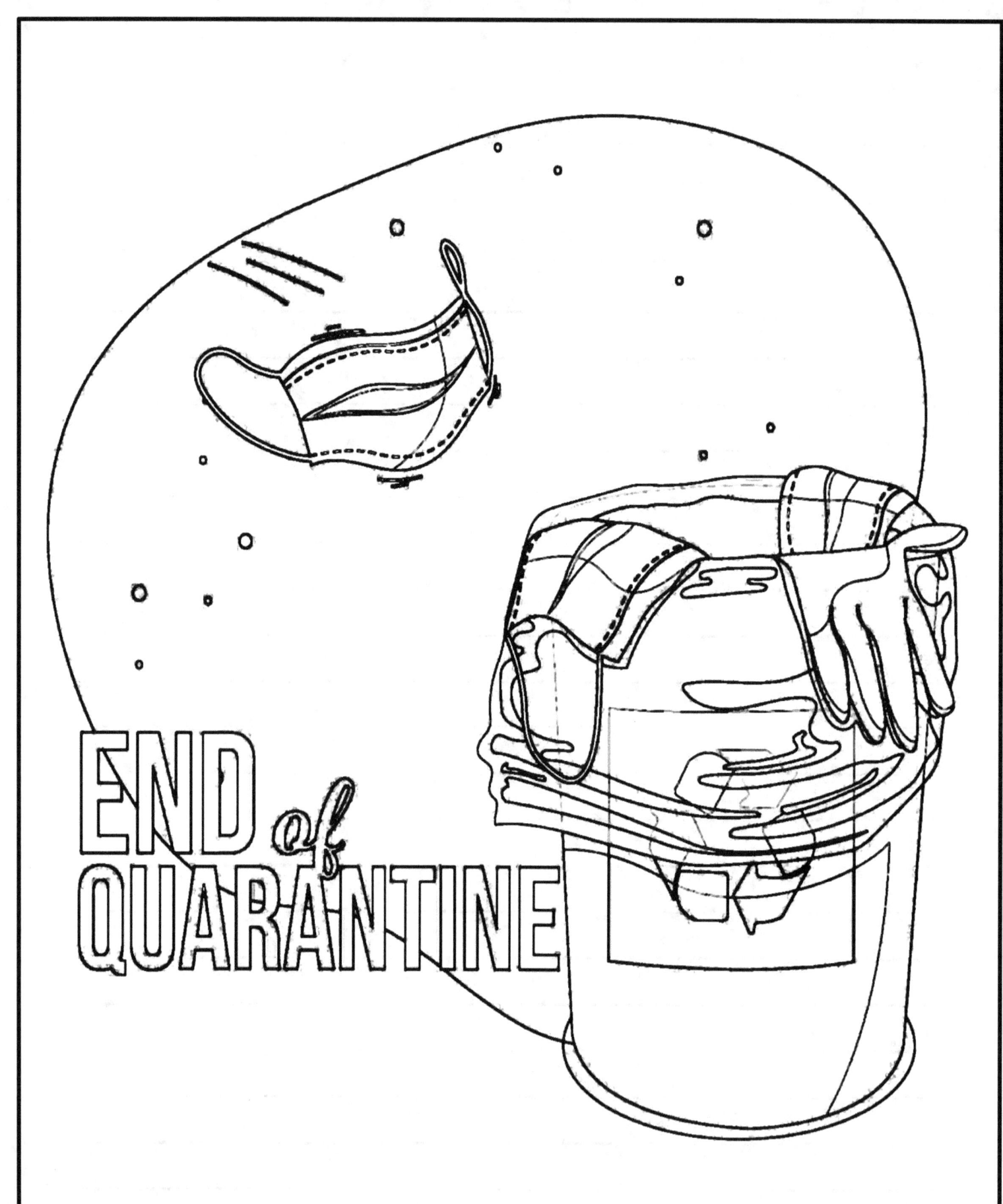

www.ingramcontent.com/pod-product-compliance
Lightning Source LLC
Chambersburg PA
CBHW080503220526
45465CB00006B/2366